Stuff About Money: No BS Financial Advice for Regular People

By Craig D. Guillot
Edited by Sandra Hume

Published by
NOLA Communications
9605 Jefferson Hwy., Ste. I #283
New Orleans, LA 70123
www.craigguillot.com

For my daughter Madeleine.

May I give you all the tools you need to succeed in life, and may you always remember that nothing is impossible.

Love, Dad

ACKNOWLEDGEMENTS

After years of hearing financial professionals talk about how poorly people manage their money, it only made sense that I write this book. I'd like to thank all of the accountants, lawyers, financial advisors, CEOs, entrepreneurs, writers, investment bankers, insurance agents and gurus I've interviewed over the years. Your collective advice, feedback, guidance and insight have not only led me to write this book, but also helped me improve my own life in more ways than you'll ever imagine. Every conversation with you is a learning experience for which I am eternally grateful. Most of you are not mentioned or sourced in this book, but if we've talked about personal finance, you have played a role.

I also thank my father for setting an example for me by being a master of living within his means. He drove his cars until they literally fell apart, never spent money on frivolous things, always looked for bargains and avoided name-brand crap. Yet he sent my sister and me to some of the best schools, always gave us more than we needed, took us on vacations and never once griped about money.

I'd like to thank my wife for putting up with my late work nights and my continuous anal talk about money… like why I need to eke out another 1.2 percent on my portfolio this year, or why we need to increase the car note payment by $63 per month to pay it off 18 months early to save $329 in interest.

Finally, I'd like to thank my editors and my peers at FreelanceSuccess.com, who have helped me build my career and thrive as a writer.

TABLE OF CONTENTS

MEET THE EXPERTS

Here are some of the experts who were interviewed for this book.

Mari Adam is president of Adam Financial Associates, Inc. and has been a practicing Certified Financial Planner for twenty years. She is a Chartered Retirement Planning Counselor and has served as the president and director of the South Florida chapter of the Financial Planning Association. She has been a guest author and commentator for such publications as *BusinessWeek*, CBS Market Watch, *The Wall Street Journal* and *Kiplinger's Personal Finance*.

Jude Boudreaux is the founder of Upperline Financial Planning in New Orleans. He is a former conference chair and president of the Financial Planning Association NexGen.

Sonya Britt is the president of the Financial Therapy Association.

Nancy Butler, a Certified Financial Planner and Certified Divorce Financial Analyst, is founder of Above All Else, Success in Life and Business, an organization helping individuals improve their bottom line. She has been quoted in publications such as *USA Today* and has been a speaker for corporations including Pfizer, General Dynamics and Dow Chemical.

Chris DesBarres is co-owner of Help Unlimited, Inc., a daily money management service that helps clients manage their personal finances in regards to paying bills, tracking insurance claims, organizing files and safeguarding important financial documents.

Howard Dvorkin is the founder of Consolidated Credit Counseling Services, Inc. and the author of *Credit Hell: How to Dig Out of Debt*.

Ethan Ewing is president of Bills.com and has nearly twenty years in the financial services industry.

Alex Forrest is vice president of AC Forrest Insurance Group in Greenville, SC.

Kimberly Foss is a Certified Financial Planner and personal finance expert with almost thirty years of industry experience. She is the founder of Empyrion Wealth Management and counsels clients on retirement, financial planning, investment management and college planning.

Michael Friedmann is a Management Consultant and creator of the economics blog The Behaviorist. Michael has tutored economics students at the college and graduate levels, in addition to working in corporate finance and economic research roles for IBM, Citizens Bank and The Kogod School of Business in Washington, D.C.

Bill Hammer, Jr., is a Certified Financial Planner and a co-founder of the Hammer Wealth Group. He is the author of *The Seven Secrets of Extraordinary Investors* and a regular contributor to *Financial Advisor Publications*.

Robert Henderson is president of Lansdowne Wealth Management, LLC. He has a B.S. in Accounting from Bentley University and earned the Accredited Asset Management Specialist (AAMS) designation from the College for Financial Planning.

Leah Ingram is the author of *Suddenly Frugal: How to Live Happier and Healthier for Less*. She shares daily tips on saving money and living frugally at Livingfrugal.com.

Patrick Killelea runs Patrick.net, one of the most widely-read blogs on the housing crash. Because he has no background in real estate, he says he will not lie to readers.

Danny Kofke is the author of *How to Survive on a Teacher's Salary* and *A Simple Book of Financial Wisdom: Teach Yourself and Your Kids how to Live Wealthy With Little Money*. He has appeared on the Fox Business Network, CNN Newsroom, ABC News Now and MSNBC Live.

Adam Koos is a financial advisor and president of Libertas Wealth Management. He is also a registered principal and branch manager at LPL Financial, the nation's largest independent broker/dealer.

Laura Laing is author of *Math for Grownups*.

Jeremy Maher is a former credit repair company owner who now educates consumers on credit and credit repair at MyCreditRepairTips.com.

Jennifer McDonough is an administrative assistant and mother of four who recovered her financial security and dug her and her family out of $120,000 in debt in 27 months. She documents her story at FieldofDebt.com.

Jon Pedley is vice president of product management of Bills.com. He has worked in the financial services industry with Charles Schwab and JPMorgan.

Joe Pitzl, CFP, is Director of Financial Planning for Intelligent Financial Strategies, LLC. He is heavily involved in the Financial Planning Association as the National Chairman of FPA NexGen.

Noah Rosenfarb, CPA, PFS, CDFA, is a divorce advisor with Freedom Divorce Advisors.

J.D. Roth is editor of GetRichSlowly.org, a web site that shares stories about debt elimination, saving money and practical investing. The site was names the best blog of 2011 by *Time* magazine and the most inspiring money blog by *Money* magazine.

Andrew Schrage is an editor at Moneycrashers.com. The twenty-something majored in economics at Brown University and previously worked for a hedge fund.

Billy Van Jura is owner operator of the insurance firm Birchyard, LLC.

Jeremy Vohwinkle is editor and owner of Generation X Finance and writes about Financial Planning for About.com. He is a Chartered Retirement Planning Counselor.

David Weliver publishes MoneyUnder30.com, a financial blog for starting out that reaches over 150,000 readers a month. He lives with his wife and daughter near Portland, Maine.

For more biographical information and direct links to their web sites, visit www.somestuffaboutmoney.com.

ABOUT THE AUTHOR

Craig D. Guillot is a business and personal finance writer from New Orleans, Louisiana. His articles have appeared in such publications as Entrepreneur, CNNMoney.com, Investor's Business Daily, Bankrate.com, CNBC.com, Washington Post and Miami Herald. He is a regular contributor to Interest.com, Better Investing and STORES Magazine, the monthly publication of the National Retail Federation. You can read more about his work at www.craigguillot.com.

STUFF ABOUT MONEY

"Money isn't the most important thing in life, but it's reasonably close to oxygen on the 'gotta have it' scale."

– *Zig Ziglar*, American author, salesperson and motivational speaker

There's no doubt about it. Money *is* important.

You can say money doesn't matter, but it controls more in your life than you think. It has a profound impact on just about everything in your reality, from the manner in which you enter this world to the way you leave it.

Every day, billions of people around the globe work, steal, invest, fight, kill, suffer and do whatever they can to obtain money or get more of it. Money is both the root of all evil and the root of all life. It causes stress, pain, happiness, joy, depression, jealousy and anger. People cry, laugh, shout, love and hate over it.

Money can dictate where you live, what you eat, what kind of education you'll get, what kind of career you'll have, how reliable your car is, what kind of clothes you wear, what kind of health care you get. It determines the level of comfort in your life, the size of your television, the quality of the furniture in your home, where you can go on the weekends, where you can eat dinner. Money can determine the life and future of your children.

With some exceptions, a life without money is bound to be filled with far more hardship, heartache, despair and sadness than a life with money.

This is not to say that money is everything, but it's pretty damn important. Some of the happiest people on Earth might scrimp by on certain parts of the globe on $12 a day, but I'd be willing to bet that most of them would rather have $15 or $18 a day.

The biggest thing is that money gives you *options*. In most cases, the more money you have, the more options you have. If you have $500 in the bank and make $8 an hour, you're going to have a lot fewer options than a person who has $15,000 in the bank and makes $55,000 per year.

Here in America we're having a rougher time with things. Life seems to be getting harder. People have lost billions in home equity, unemployment has been near 9 percent, gas prices are near an all-time high and the cost of health insurance is skyrocketing. And in the past 10 years we've suffered an alarming number of bubbles and stock market crashes. Wherever you stand financially, chances are your financial life is a little bit more difficult than it was a decade ago.

It's all the more reason why we have to better understand and manage the money we have, because dollars are becoming scarcer. And due to what some say could be high inflation in the coming years, those dollars may also be worth less.

There really isn't a point in life where most of us are officially taught stuff about money. They might teach us about coins in grammar school, or we might learn some basic math related to money, but no one ever teaches us about the important things. Like why we should stay out of credit card debt. Or why Roth IRAs are a good idea. Or why we should begin saving for your retirement as young as possible. Or why health insurance is essential. Instead, we're bombarded with commercials and advertisements about why you need to upgrade to the new iPad, shop at the Gap, buy that 65" television on sale at Best Buy this weekend. It almost makes you feel as if our system was designed to get you to spend. And in many ways it is. But at some point the bill is going to come due.

We can't always control how much we make, but we can control how we live and how we manage and spend our money.

Don't listen to your grandpa's crap about how he had to walk 15 miles to school each day in 20-degree weather when he was five, worked in a steel mill barefoot 73 hours a week at age 12 and then served in World War II. Yeah, shit was hard back then and people might have been a bit tougher—but things were also much simpler.

Back in 1950 one might have had a mortgage, a utility bill, cheap auto insurance and maybe a phone bill. They didn't have to save much for retirement because they had a pension and Social Security to look forward to, and they didn't spend nearly as much on health insurance.

Today, pensions don't exist, we can't be assured that Social Security is going to be there when we need it, and no one needs to tell you that health insurance costs a fortune these days. We also have a cable bills, cell phone bills, high-speed Internet bills, life insurance premiums, auto loans, high auto-insurance premiums, credit card bills, satellite radio, satellite television, gym memberships and home equity loan payments. We also need an iPod, a Wii, a big-screen television, a tablet computer, a Blu-ray player. And that doesn't even cover all the cool things our children want.

We may not technically *need* all these things, but if we want to live a middle-class lifestyle, it costs a hell of a lot more relative to your income than it did in the 1950s. Very few families sit around and play Monopoly at the dinner table anymore. The entertainment and fun we've grown accustomed to have become expensive.

We also face an economic uncertainty that few generations have had to deal with. The reality is that the rich are getting richer, the poor are getting poorer and the middle class is being increasingly pinched, with costs rising all around them while their incomes are standing still.

Few people in their 20s, 30s and 40s will have pensions. Most will be laid off at least twice, switch jobs up to eight times, change health care carriers every few years and likely go through a few economic hardships.

But we do have some good things going for us: Interest rates are low, stock market returns have been reasonable, and our technology allows us to handle our personal finances in ways that we never could before.

And that technology is unbelievable. Think about the fact that in the 80s, we'd do the family budgeting on a columned notepad and would have to drive down to a stockbroker's office to invest in the market. Nowadays, we can check your account balances, pay the bills, have access to all of our finances and even trade stocks on our cell phones—while sitting on the toilet. But   our   relationship with money is also changing. We buy more, we save less, we put more on credit cards, we take out bigger mortgages for bigger homes, we buy fancier cars and we're more interested in name brands and style than practicality. At least more than previous generations were.

Our material expectations have risen and our current societal norms place a higher emphasis on spending than they do saving. Our cost of housing is far higher relative to our incomes than it was in the past. The list of what's stacked against us goes on and on.

Health insurance seems to be a ticking time bomb in this nation. Health care costs keep going up, insurance premiums keep rising and Americans are spending a larger portion of their incomes on health care. A typical middle-class family with individual coverage now spends a whopping 22 percent of their household income on health care. Those with employer-based coverage spend an average of 8 percent of their income on health-care costs. And the less you make, the more it hurts.

Think about the fact that most people spend more on health care than they contribute to their savings and retirement funds. It sucks.

All of this bad news means that we are going to have to manage our money better, learn to do more with less and learn to creatively find ways to make it in the future. One would think that we'd put an emphasis on effective money management, but we don't. While everything in our financial lives has become so much more complicated, our comprehension of personal finance hasn't improved. As a society, we're probably *less* savvy about money than we were back in the 1970s.

I've written this book because in the hundreds of financial professionals I've interviewed and countless personal finance articles I've written over the years, barely an interview has gone by where at least in some point of the conversation we didn't talk about the lack of financial literacy in America.

Don't think for a second that I'm wealthy or have a massive income. I don't have a million bucks in the bank, I don't live in a big house, there isn't a fancy car in my driveway, and you're not going to see me retiring at age 50.

I'm a regular Joe just like you. But I have developed a solid financial discipline over the years, and I've had the privilege of speaking with a wide spectrum of financial professionals. I've set realistic expectations for myself and developed a loose financial philosophy that I can live with for the rest of my life. I'm fairly happy, I can buy anything I need—and I rarely, if ever, worry about money. I live within my means and I maintain my financial life through careful and smart money management. I may not do it all, but I know what to do. And throughout this book I'll give it to you straight. No bullshit.

Keep in mind that not everything here may apply to you. Maybe you can't implement every single piece of advice. But you can do something—and something is a start. Understand this: Financial strength and stability is not an all-or-nothing game. If you can't save $20,000, then save $10,000. If you can't save that, then save $5,000. At the end of the day, something is better than nothing. Even $500 is still better than $100. Ten percent is great, but if you can only get 7 percent, take it. If not that, then 3 percent. See what I mean?

And when it comes to debt, it's best to have none, of course, but having a little is certainly better than having a lot. No one wants to be paying off $2,000 in credit card debt at 15 percent, but that sure as hell beats trying to tackle $9,500 in credit card debt at 22 percent.

In the perfect world of Dave Ramsey and Suze Orman's financial advice, you would contribute $5,000 to your Roth IRA every year, add $2,000 to your child's ESA or 529, have no car note, no credit card debt and a 15-year mortgage where you are making an additional monthly principal payment every year. While that's good advice, their standards can be hard to live up to. Most people will try it for a month or two, then fall off the wagon because it just becomes too hard and they feel they're sacrificing too much.

You can't be 100 percent debt-free, max out your retirement accounts and save 50 percent of your income on $40,000 per year unless you're eating Ramen noodles every night. And do you really want to skimp by and pinch every penny until you're 68 so that you can retire with $3 million? You may not even live that long. What if you plan to start living life at age 60—and die at 55? Find a middle ground and do what you can.

Maybe you pay off that $800 in credit card debt, then put $2,500 in your Roth, $1,000 in your child's IRA and another $1,200 towards your emergency savings. That may be all you can do for the year without having to give up your life. You still want to go out to eat once in a while, you still want to take a little family vacation to the beach. Well, do it. Do the best you can. Meet these financial goals halfway if you must; it's better than nothing. Even if you meet only half of your financial goals, there mere fact that you *have* goals and are working towards them puts you well ahead of the pack.

Get the picture? You don't have to be perfect. No one is. All you have to do is the best that you can, and if you at least try to implement some of these rules, you'll be headed in the right direction. The key word is *improve.* And with so many cards and odds stacked against you these days, any financial improvement can make a difference in your life. Every little improvement you make, every dollar you pay off in debt, every dollar you put away for retirement is going to pay off in multiple ways later on. The extra $100 you put away today could be worth $1,700 30 years from now, and the extra $100 you put towards paying off a debt could save you $500 down the line. All this stuff snowballs with time.

Remember that all financial milestones are made with baby steps. The retiree who has $1.4 million in his IRA likely didn't land massive sums of money to get where he was. Chances are he or she started building that wealth back in their 20s with small contributions of $50 or $100. They built that sum month by month, year by year, dollar by dollar, paycheck by paycheck, dividend by dividend over time since they started working. And they did so not necessarily because they had a big income or made great investment decisions, but because they made a plan and a commitment to building their assets—and they did it.

If you don't have an IRA, open one now. Even if you already have a 401(k) at work, open one. Just do it. It's hard to get started, but once you do it becomes easier. That first $25 may seem pathetic, but before you know it you'll have $500 in there. Then you'll hit $1,000 and feel as if you've turned a corner. And it builds from there. The coolest thing is that as your savings grows, the progress inspires you to save even more. Interest, dividends and capital gains add even further to the mix.

It is widely said that the first $100,000 is the hardest to save. When you're starting out and have $1,000 in your account, an 8 percent annual return will give you only $1,080 the next year. Earning $80 over the course of a year isn't very motivating. But when you've got $100,000 and you're earning 8 percent, that's $8,000 you'll earn... for doing absolutely nothing. And due to compound interest, where you earn interest on your interest that grows your money even faster, it can happen quickly. The year after that, you'd have $116,640 in your account, and by year three you'd have $125,971. Within eight years, you'd have $200,000 and have earned $100,000 on your money. So while it may take you twenty years to sock away that first hundred grand, you could get the next hundred grand free in only eight years. If you kept contributing and continuing the trend the interest would stack up the funds even more, making your earnings higher than ever.

This underlines why it's important to get a grip on your finances and start managing your money properly as early as you can. The sooner you can bank more money, the sooner your money can start making its own money. You're bound to make some big financial mistakes in your 20s, but the sooner you can break from that and develop some common-sense productive financial habits, the better off you're going to be. Continue making these mistakes in your 30s and beyond, and you're going to run into some serious problems in your life. If haven't improved your financial decision-making by the time you're in your 40s (and many people haven't), you're likely only a decade or two from the house falling down on you.

Just do your best.

Financial strength and security is also not about having a big house, fancy cars and material luxuries. There are some people that have all of these things but are in debt up to their eyeballs, so they have little security. They might have a $350,000 house, drive a $65,000 BMW, and wear a $10,000 Rolex on their wrist, but a look at their balance sheet may well tell you they're $400,000 in debt, have little more than $12,000 in liquid assets, have no retirement accounts, and don't even carry health insurance. On the outside this person might appear to have it all, but on the inside, they've got a net worth that's less than that of the one-toothed homeless man you see begging for change on the corner. The problem with this is that while people like this may have some nice material possessions, their heavy debt means they're living on borrowed time. At some point they're going to have to pay that massive bill.

Being financially strong means cutting through the bullshit, living within your means, having little or no debt and managing to put a reasonable portion of your income aside every month. It's not outside your reach. You can have financial strength if you're making only $30,000 per year, and you can have it if you've got only a few thousand bucks in the bank. It's all relative to your lifestyle and the money decisions that you make on a daily basis.

Start with the basic concept of, first, learning to live within your means; second, staying out of debt; and third, saving the difference. These three simple actions alone will do more to boost your financial security than anything else. But it's not as simple as it may sound. Even if you're doing everything right, one layoff, bad stroke of luck or sickness can drive you into debt. Stuff happens, and before you know it you're left with nothing to save. While you can't always control those things, you can put yourself in a position to better handle emergencies. That's why you should save and have some money put aside strictly for emergencies.

Next, think about the two biggest expenses you'll likely have: where you live and what you drive. If you buy a house and drive a car that you can really afford, it could set the stage for financial prosperity. On the other hand, if you spend too much on your house and/or your car, you could end up sabotaging your financial future. It sounds simple, but it's one of the biggest detractors of wealth in America: If you're spending 60 percent of your gross income on your home and vehicles, that doesn't leave much for things like food, fun and most importantly, savings and debt payments.

Understand that financial strength and stability don't happen overnight. You can't make a few changes in your life and have a complete turnaround the next day—or even the next week or the next month. Your financial life is a marathon. If you're sprinting at mile 2 you won't even make it to mile 10, and just because you have a leg pain at mile 14 doesn't mean you won't make it to mile 20. You need to keep your eye on the prize: mile 26.2. Maintain a slow, steady pace.

Financial strength and stability is also a state of mind. You have to think about it, be conscious of it and know how every financial decision you make can impact it in the long run. You have to be able to say that you can't afford something. You have to be able to walk away from name-brand or fancy stuff, and you have to be willing to forego what some conspicuous consumers might call the finer things in life. This doesn't mean you can't have the very occasional splurge, you just have to look in the mirror, be honest with yourself and learn to live on the income you earn.

This is not a book about saving money. We're not going to tell you how to clip coupons, spot bargains, shop at secondhand stores and save 31 percent on the newest gadgets. All of those things are great and can certainly contribute to your financial strength by reducing your spending, but I want to show you bigger and better tactics to improve your finances.

You can shop for clothes at Goodwill, clip coupons and look for all the sales you want, but if you're doing that while throwing away $600 per month on a car note, you're really just running on a treadmill. All those savings you have coming in the front door are going out the back door. Cutting back spending in one spot so you can spend more in another doesn't reduce spending; it merely displaces it.

This book is also realistic. If maximizing your IRA and paying off your 60-month car loan in only eleven months means you have to give up your life, then what's the point? I don't want you to live poor to save money. You can do all you want to prepare for the future, but it's all for nothing if you can't live and have a little fun in the present.

Stuff About Money wants you to find that middle ground that is best for you. You may have to sacrifice some things, but you don't have to sacrifice everything. Instead of that $5,000 trip to Tahiti, you take a $2,000 trip to Mexico and then bank the $3,000 difference. Perhaps you forego that $28,000 new SUV for a pre-owned one from the year before that has only 7,000 miles on the odometer and costs $22,000. Hey, you're still living a decent life, you're just doing it for less money and still managing to save for your future. That's because instead of fretting about saving $.55 on a box of cookies, you're constantly making decisions about big purchases that are saving you big bucks. One good decision on buying a new car could be worth more than years of coupon clipping and saving.

You also need to cut yourself a break at times and use small splurges to reward yourself for the positive behavior. Did you scrimp and work hard to pay off $5,000 in credit card debt in the past year? Awesome. Now save for a few more months and get yourself something nice or take a weekend trip. Don't deprive yourself. It's important to make the right decisions and budget cuts, but if you try to live on a shoestring for too long without having a little fun here and there, you're likely not going to make it. You should be able to enjoy your life, and if you're clamping down too hard on yourself you might fall back into your old ways.

If there is one good thing that has come from the recession, is it that Americans are starting to come around. It may be happening slowly, but more and more people are realizing the dangers of living in debt. According to the Federal Reserve Bank of New York, total household debt, through payment or default, fell by $1.1 trillion, or 8.6 percent, between mid-2008 and mid-2011.

Then again, Americans may be not be intentionally shying away from debt; they may just be finding it harder to borrow. It's a lot more difficult these days to buy a house with a 2 percent down payment or a car with no money down. Credit card companies have increased their standards a bit and aren't quite giving away plastic like it's candy anymore. The Credit Card Reform Act of 2009 has instituted some reform that requires credit card companies to show the true costs of lending and paying the minimum balance. Those who take the time to look at their statements are finding out that the monthly $52 they're paying on their $2,600 balance is barely doing anything to pay down the principal. They can now see that if they continue to make that minimum payment, they won't get rid of their credit card debt for 17 years. And by that time they'll have paid $1,800 in interest.

There's no telling how long this mild aversion to debt could last. It may just be temporary. If the economy turns around by 2015 and consumers feel better about themselves, they may start digging themselves into a hole again. They may go back down to Walmart with their Visa to buy the newest gadgets and gizmos.

Whatever the case, you don't want to be a part of this. You want to stay level-headed and think more about your long-term financial future and health than about what kind of cool crap your neighbor just bought. Everything indicates that life is going to get harder, so be prepared to manage your money a little better.

I've pulled pieces of advice and some stuff about money from almost three dozen financial professionals to come up with some of the best ways to improve your financial life. Some of these tips are common-sense, time-tested rules that have been proven to build wealth. Like staying out of debt—everyone knows you're supposed to do it, but few actually make the effort and sacrifice to accomplish it. Others, like figuring out how much you need to save for retirement or knowing when to refinance your home, are a little more complex. Overall, these tips come together to help you change the way you think about your money and your financial future.

This is also not a "how to get rich" book. While you could certainly put yourself on a track to accumulating wealth by implementing some of the tips in this book, I can't teach you how to start some magic business or follow the rainbow to the big pot of gold waiting on the other end. Let's be real. It's highly unlikely that you're going to come up with a no-fail business idea that makes you millions over the next three years. We can't teach you how to do that, and neither can the person who claims he can if you just buy his $15 book. Sure, you can dream about it, but it's not going to happen.

Don't let it stop you from trying, of course, but realistically, chances are slim that you're ever going to be "rich." You're probably going to work about thirty years, making around $50,000 a year. You'll likely drive a regular car for the rest of your life. You're going to wonder if you're ever going to have enough money to retire, or if your health insurance is ever going to stop going up, or when you might ever be able to afford that dream trip.

And there are a lot of things that you'll never do and will never experience because you just don't have that much money. You're a regular Joe or Jane, just like me.

The good news is that if you play your cards right, you still can live a decent life within your means. You can take vacations; you can sleep at night without having to worry about money; you *can* have a life with a modest level of financial security.

What this book does deliver is a mixture of financial tips and advice that that, when applied properly, can put you on the right track towards improving your financial strength and stability.

I also try to avoid using the word "wealth." Wealth is typically defined as "an abundance of valuable material possessions or resources" or a "great amount." The problem with that is that wealth is all relative to your age, lifestyle, income and location. For a 30-year-old living in west Texas, earning $65,000 per year and having $45,000 in the bank might constitute a fair level of wealth. But for a family of four in San Francisco, a household income of $105,000 per year and $85,000 in the bank is likely far from wealth. "Wealth" is all in the eye of the beholder. One man's vision of wealth could be another man's vision of the poorhouse. What you want to build isn't wealth, it's *security*. You want to build that financial strength that is just right for you, that gives you enough to pay your bills, put some money away for your future and sleep soundly at night without fear of whether or not you'll be able to pay the mortgage next month.

You probably won't be rich but you can be happy and secure—which is worth a whole lot more.

CHAPTER 1

THE ROOF OVER YOUR HEAD

"Owner-occupied homes will always be the basis for healthy and stable neighborhoods. But coming generations need to realize that while houses are possessions and part of a good life, they are not always good investments on the road to financial independence."

—*Robert Bridges*, Professor of Clinical Finance and Business Economics at the University of Southern California's Marshall School of Business.

Buying a home is not just about having enough to pay the mortgage. It's about having enough *after you pay the mortgage* to cover everything else.

How much you spend on your home relative to how much you make is one of the biggest decisions that will impact your finances. Three, ten, even twenty years from now, all kinds of financial metrics will be dependent on the proportion of your income you are, and were, spending on your mortgage. How much you put down, how much your mortgage is and the interest rate you pay will directly affect how much you have left to pay for other things in your life—arguably more important things like retirement savings, your children's education, your emergency fund or simple debt reduction.

As a general rule of thumb you should not spend more than 28 percent of your income on the mortgage. This includes not just principal and interest but maintenance, property taxes and insurance. When you go over this limit—and many Americans do—you're going to make it harder to cover other financial obligations.

"I see it with people at all income levels who buy too much house, and it becomes like a noose around their neck. I'd rather see people buy a house they can afford, stay in it a long time and fund the hell out of their retirement accounts," says financial planner Bill Hammer.

David Weliver, publisher of MoneyUnder30.com, says the problem with spending too much on a home is that it limits your asset diversification. That's because if you don't have enough left over at the end of the month to invest in your retirement or liquid assets, your home will eventually become your primary and only asset. That's okay and common when you're 30, but it's not an ideal picture to be 60 years old with your house being your biggest asset.

Ideally you want to have money in three places: your house, a savings account or two and the stock market. Millions of homeowners found out in the 2007 and 2008 housing crash that banking on the house was a pretty shitty idea.

"People found out the hard way that when things went bad in that one market, they lost not only their entire 'investment,' but their place to live," says Weliver. "You want to have enough diversification in your financial life. It's all about moderation and diversification."

Many say a house is like an anchor that gives you financial stability and security, helping to set you up for long-term wealth appreciation, at least more than if you rent. While that is true, it can also be an anchor that can weigh you down in poverty or a life less than you should be living.

If it's too big relative to your income, that monthly payment can detract from building liquid savings. And just because a person has a nice big house doesn't mean they have money to back it up. Many Americans live in a façade, a house of cards where the only thing behind it is a mountain of debt and little cash or liquid assets.

In recent years, millions of Americans have finally woken to the danger of this situation. According to Zillow, almost 30 percent of American homes are "underwater" in their mortgages, meaning the homeowners owe more than the home is worth. Think about it: Not only do they not "own" their home, they're not even close to owning it because they actually owe the bank 10 percent more than the thing is worth. And if that many people are underwater, how many more have little equity in their homes? Can we guess another 20 percent? That would mean *half* of all American home-owners have little or no equity in their homes.

This underlines why people should never buy a primary home as "an investment." It is first and foremost a place to live and raise a family. Far down the list—*way* down the list—it is a poor, and at best mediocre, "investment." We'll get to that later in this chapter.

"People were just getting too hyped up into thinking their home was an investment. If you plan to downsize in the future when you retire, that's one thing, but your home should never be seen as an investment," says Kimberly Foss, founder of the Empyrion Wealth Institute. "Buy a home because it's a nice place to live, and then you work to pay off the mortgage. That's it."

Also, don't fall for the myth that your monthly note can't change. It's true that if you do have a 30-year fixed-rate mortgage, your principal and interest payments won't change, but your property taxes and insurance certainly will. In many parts of the country property taxes are actually rising, as local governments struggle to maintain tax revenues where housing values have plummeted.

The cost of your house can also increase because of mainte-nance. And if you live in an area susceptible to hurricanes or tor-nadoes, you likely know very well that the cost of insurance can skyrocket after large disasters. Homeowners insurance premiums are expected to rise further in 2012 due to an increasing number of natural disasters in 2011.

If you're like many Americans, you may already be in a house that you can not afford. It doesn't matter how you got to this point, all that matters is where you go from here. Maybe you can't sell and downsize because the value of your home has fallen so much over the past few years that you're nearly underwater in your mortgage, if not already there. If you sell now, you're going to lock in a massive loss on your home and having nothing left.

So what do you do when you owe $220,000 on a home that is only worth $190,000? The answer is as complex as the IRS tax code and all depends on your situation. The options range from staying put and waiting for a rebound in housing prices to walking away and facing a voluntary foreclosure.

It may sound like a radical idea, but especially in this day and age, some people aren't meant to be homeowners. There's nothing wrong with that. Owning a home is not a necessity for living a fulfilling life. In many parts of the country, especially in higher-priced markets, people will go their entire lives without ever owning a home. They will happily rent forever and be satisfied doing so because in those markets, the cost to rent may be far cheaper than the cost to own. One has to factor in that when renting is cheaper than buying, the difference can be invested to actually make a profit that is more than a house would be worth.

"Today I don't think everyone should buy a home. It is just not for everyone. You need to have a down payment that gives you skin in the game, [and] you need to not overspend or it could be a financial disaster, worse than had you just rented," says Foss.

Think carefully about your options to buy versus renting. Base your decision on formulas and financial principles, not emotion. The commonly-said phrases "real estate always goes up" and "your house is your best investment" have totally been debunked in the past few years: Between 2006 and late 2011, real estate values nationwide fell by more than 30 percent.

It won't be this way forever, but in a non-HGTV–fueled standard credit market, the long-term appreciation of real estate is only 1 or 2 percent above inflation. That's 4 to 6 percent, not the 15 to 20 percent people were used to at the dysfunctional point in history when they thought granite countertops were "an investment" in their long-term financial future.

Live in your house, just don't take it too seriously as an investment. Any gains you may eventually earn by selling it or anything else you do should be considered icing on the cake of your real investments: your retirement fund and liquid assets. Throughout this book we'll lay out dozens of reasons why and will point out all the other places you should be spreading some of your money.

Haven't bought a home yet? If you can afford to make a down payment of 20 percent, can squeeze in the housing costs with less than 28 percent of your income and plan to stay in the house a long time, then it might be a good decision to buy. If not, you should seriously consider your long-term financial future before jumping in.

Know when to buy and when to rent

Traditional real-estate advice contends that rent is "throwing away money" and that you should buy a house as soon as you're financially able. There was a time when that might have been the case, but in today's constantly changing environment where people are frequently moving, real estate values are plummeting, rents are declining and the housing market has been artificially inflated for almost a decade, that's not necessarily true.

It's all dependent on your own personal situation

There is no one-size-fits-all equation. If and when you should buy a house depends on the cost of owning versus renting in your community, how much you have for a down payment, how stable your job is and how much of an emergency fund you have. There are times when buying a house is a great financial move and times when it could be a catastrophic mistake. Do the math and determine what the best choice is for you, without outside advice. Real estate agents, friends and family may not know the full extent of your financial situation and your future plans and goals.

Financial planner Mari Adam says if you're struggling to come up with the cash for a closing, it's a good indicator that you may not be prepared. You should have at least six mortgage payments tucked away in another fund to cover things like maintenance, repairs and any insurance deductibles you might have to cover. Recommendations for annual maintenance costs run from 1.5 to 4 percent of the purchase price. So if you're buying a $200,000 home, you should plan to have $3,000 to $8,000 per year on hand to cover those expenses.

"You really need a cash cushion before you buy. The reality of owning a home is that you have taxes, insurance, floods, leaks, the air conditioner, the roof. It can get expensive," says Adam.

When homeowners jump in without cash on hand, their only solution is to resort to credit cards or a home equity loan or line of credit. Adam says it's a bad idea to buy a home if you're living paycheck to paycheck (or will be after you buy the home) because you'll be one step from disaster. You also might want to rent if you are planning on moving in the next few years because the transaction costs alone (closing costs for the purchase, realtor commission for the sale) will be take a big bite out of your bank account.

Patrick Killelea of Patrick.net, one of the most widely-read blogs on the ongoing housing crash, says the decision on when to buy should always be weighed against the cost of renting. He points out that in many places it is cheaper to rent than own a house equivalent in size and quality. If annual rents are 2.5 percent of the purchase price when mortgage rates are 5 percent, he says it costs twice as much to borrow the money as it does to borrow the house. He says the true sign of a bottom is when the price is low enough that you could rent out the house and make a profit. You can calculate what he calls the "buying safety" rule by dividing the annual rent by the purchase price. In that calculation, 3 percent means "do not buy," 6 percent is "borderline" and 9 percent means "okay to buy" because prices are reasonable. Killelea says that as a general rule, it is okay to buy a house when it is cheaper to own than rent over a seven-year period.

"The price of the house compared to renting is critical. It is amazing how many people just ignore the price [of a house] because they are paying with borrowed money," says Killelea. "Most people act on emotion rather than math. If math fits with what they do, they look at it, if not, they ignore it.".

You can find some good rent vs. buy calculators at Lending Tree and Bankrate.com. Make a decision that is right for you—not what happens to be right for your friend, parents or relatives.

The choice between buying and renting is not purely financial. Owing a home is an entire lifestyle change from renting. There are a lot of factors and responsibilities that come into play when you own a house. Maintenance and repairs will mean paying bills you never had to pay as a tenant. Are you willing to mow the yard during the summer? Are you ready to face an $800 repair bill when your hot water heater craps out? How about staying home all weekend to repaint the bedrooms? Or leaving yourself open to financial responsibility for the damages from a natural disaster?

Houses aren't just expensive, they can also be a hassle and eat up a lot of your time. When you are a homeowner and have a problem, you either have to pay a lot of money for someone to handle it or you can spend your own time handling it yourself. Carefully consider this before jumping in and understand that it may not be the right choice for you.

Finally, don't buy a house if you're planning to move in a few years. The closing costs when you buy and the realtor commissions when you sell could easily eat up any appreciation in price that you may have earned over the years. David Weliver, publisher of MoneyUnder30.com, said you should never buy a home because you "think it's an investment." We'll elaborate in the next few pages on why that is. Buy a home first and foremost because it makes financial sense and because it's a nice place to live and raise a family, not because you think it will appreciate in value and you'll be able to sell it later for a profit.

Don't buy more house than you can afford

If you decide it's the right move for you to buy a house, be careful not to overspend. Jeremy Vohwinkle of Gen X Finance says that despite the recent housing crash, many Americans have a desire to buy more house than they can afford. But just because the bank will loan you the money and just because you can barely swing the note doesn't mean you should max out your lending capacity. Many Americans got in over their heads in the early and mid-2000s and found out the hard way through foreclosures and short sales that they bit off more than they could chew.

Don't spend more than 28 percent of your monthly income on your house

Most lenders and financial advisers recommend that you not spend more than 28 percent of your monthly income on your housing. If you have a household income of $70,000, for example, you shouldn't be spending more than $1,633 per month on your house note. This includes the cost of your homeowners insurance, flood insurance and property taxes, which are usually held in escrow. If those items total $500, that means you should spend only $1,133 on principal and interest.

Sometimes lenders will let you go over this percentage, but in any case, avoid buying the most expensive house you can technically afford. Doing so compromises meeting other financial goals like retirement, savings, college funds and other investments.

It will be more difficult to save for your future

Buying more house than you can afford means you're essentially giving up other important assets and things in your financial life so you can swing the cost of the home. "You're going to put some of your other financials on hold because that money is going to be funneled into the house. If you save $500 per month on your mortgage, that's more than enough to max out your IRA every year," says Vohwinkle.

You might be surprised to discover that 28 percent of your monthly income may not buy you the house you were expecting, but if you want to go on vacations, have fun on the weekends, retire someday, send your kids to college and enjoy some things in life outside of the four walls of your house, you may have to settle for something in a price range that's more financially sensible.

If you can't put 20 percent down, you probably can't afford it

Kimberly Foss says you also shouldn't be buying a home if you can't afford a 20 percent down payment on it. So many first-time homeowners stretch to make their down payment and cover the mortgage thinking that they'll get a raise or make more money in the future, but it doesn't always happen. Others make that stretch thinking the value of their home will rise and then they'll be able to sell it for a profit or create a cash cushion with a home equity loan. But *hope* is not a financial plan.

"Don't overbuy and get emotionally attached to what you think the house is worth. Most people overbought during the boom because it was just too easy. The bill will come home to roost at some point," says Foss.

You're setting yourself up for disaster

The biggest risk with living so close to the edge is that you're that much closer to disaster. Stuff happens. Your or your partner could get in a car accident. You could come down with brain cancer. You might have to care for your aging mother. At that point, you'll wish you had the extra $400 per month you're now spending because you had to have the house with the pool and the elaborate marble bathroom. David Weliver says that spending too much on a house can put you in a dangerously precarious situation where you're only one step away from disaster or credit card debt.

"If you don't have enough money left after paying the mortgage to save for the future, you're setting yourself up for disaster. And there's no security in that," says Weliver.

No one is saying you can't have these things or that you have to sell yourself short, it's just that you have to learn to live with the income you're making and the money you have. Unless your plan is to downsize to a storage shed when you're older, you're likely not going to see any money that you put into your house.

"The money you put into a house is not going to be there until you sell it. And when you sell it, you might do so at a lot less than what you paid for it. You don't want to put all of your money into a house and not save for your future," says Weliver.

Know what to do if you're underwater in your mortgage

One out of three of you reading this may very well be underwater in your mortgage. It means you owe more on your house than it's worth. It's a shitty situation to be in. Think about it. You owe *more* than what your home is worth. So what are your options?

Stay where you are

If you don't have to move for a while for any particular reason and don't have any problems paying the mortgage, then don't do anything. If you owe only 10 percent more than you're home is worth, there's a fair chance you'll be back in the black in three to five years. Experts say we could still have a few tough years ahead in the housing market. The long-term historical average annual growth of real estate is about 3 percent. Understand that your borrowing might also be limited by the fact that you are underwater in your mortgage. Don't plan on getting a second mortgage or HELOC anytime soon.

Refinance through government programs

If you don't want to wait for your house's value to rebound or are having trouble making your payments, consider refinancing through a government program. The Home Affordable Refinance Program (HARP) was originally supposed to help 5 million borrowers qualify for cheaper mortgages. But by last fall only 900,000 homes had been refinanced through the program because homeowners weren't allowed to borrow more than 125 percent of the value of their homes. That led President Barack Obama to scrap the cap. You can now apply for a new loan no matter how much you owe or what your home is currently worth.

Another option is to refinance through the Federal Housing Administration. Some of its refi programs will rewrite your mortgage regardless of how much—or how little—equity you may have. Some borrowers may also find it easier to obtain an FHA loan because you can have lower credit scores and more debt than non-FHA mortgages allow. In some instances you can even qualify if you're currently unemployed—something that's impossible to do anywhere else.

Ask your lender for a short sale

You could also ask your lender about a short sale. This is when the bank agrees to accept a sales price on the property of less than you owe on your mortgage and forgives the remaining debt. Lenders are only willing to do this when they'll lose less money than they would if you default and must foreclose on a property. Short sales are always a long and arduous process. You'll need a real estate agent and attorney to help you see it through to a successful conclusion.

Be aware that a short sale will really hurt your credit. In most cases, it will show up on your credit as pre-foreclosure or redemption status and can result in a dip of 100 to 300 points in your credit score. If you managed to do a short sale and didn't miss any payments, you might get lucky and buy another home immediately. But if you did miss payments, you could have to wait up to two years or more to buy another home.

There could also be tax ramifications in the "loan forgiveness" that the bank may grant you. If you had a $230,000 mortgage and the bank let you sell the house for $200,000 and forgave $30,000, you could owe taxes on that difference.

Rent it out

If you need to move, renting could be an option. There's a lot of work to it, both legally and financially, and it can also be a hassle. You'll likely need to consult a lawyer or accountant and will need a new insurance policy on the property. You'll also have to establish a market rental rate that covers the mortgage, insurance, taxes, legal costs and property management fees. You may not find a tenant willing to pay as much as you'd like, but if your only other option is letting the house sit vacant, some rent is better than no rent. When selecting a tenant you cannot discriminate on the basis of race, religion or sexual orientation, but you can and should use credit checks, background checks and references.

Walk away

Finally, if you can't pay the mortgage, are falling into delinquency and are nearing foreclosure, there is the option to walk away. It' not something anyone would be proud to do, but it may be the only choice when you owe more than a home is worth. That's because by walking away, you stop the bleeding. At this point you're already neck-deep so walking out on your mortgage can at least stop the fall before it's over your head.

"Walking away isn't advisable for pride reasons, but if you're that deep in the hole it may be the only option, especially if you don't plan on buying a home for the next five to seven years," said Adam Koos, president of Libertas Wealth Management.

And don't think that you'll be the only one walking out on your mortgage. It has become a choice for so many people that there's even a Web site, Youwalkaway.com, that can help you through every step of the process. The company has already helped more than 7,000 homeowners go through the process of foreclosure, short sale or simply walking away. If you decide to take this route, do it as carefully as possible because it will impact your credit score and you might not be able to buy another home for a while.

Make an extra mortgage payment per year...or not

Making an extra mortgage payment every year can save you tens of thousands of dollars in interest over the course of your loan. It can also help you pay off your home much faster so that you can start putting more money towards better things like your liquid savings and retirement accounts. Making one extra mortgage payment per year on a 20-year loan could mean paying it off in as little as 17 years; do the same for a 30-year loan, and you could pay it off in as little as 24 years.

Take care of higher-cost debts first

Consider making an extra mortgage payment only if your emergency fund is in place, along with any savings you'll need. Even more importantly, you should have no other outstanding debts such as credit card, a home equity loan or an auto loan at a higher interest rate. Generally speaking, it will save you more money to pay down higher-cost debts with higher interest rates first. If you're carrying credit card debt in particular, don't even think about making extra mortgage payments until that's paid off, not just because the interest rate is so high, but because that interest rate can go up at any moment. At least your mortgage rate is fixed for 30 years. It's pointless to put additional funds towards paying off a fixed mortgage at 6 percent when you're carrying $13,000 in credit card debt at 20 percent or an $8,000 car loan at 9 percent.

Factor other investment opportunities

Finally, you may also want to weigh making extra payments against any possible investment opportunities that you may have. If you bought a house or refinanced in 2010 and 2011, you may be paying near 4 percent on your mortgage. That is so low that you may be better off carrying that debt and using your excess cash to fund some investments that may bring you a higher return. The interest rate you're paying should be weighed against the interest rate you can earn. If you can buy into a stock that's paying a dividend of 5.5 percent and you're willing to sit on it for 10 or 20 years, you may be better off doing that rather than putting that extra money towards your mortgage. Of course, you could lose money in the stock market but many might argue there's a lot more upside.

Koos said some people get a large emotional reward out of paying off their mortgage. There's a certain sense of security one can get from knowing that their home is completely paid for. You'll likely want to try to pay off your home by the time you retire, but do the math to see what makes the best financial sense for you.

"You might be able to sleep better at night with no mortgage. But if you're in the 25 percent tax bracket and have a 4 percent rate on your mortgage, that's really only 3 percent," says Koos.

Koos said that some people who are determined to pay off their mortgage as quickly as possible may opt for a 15-year loan. But with the marginal difference in interest rates between a 15-year and 30-year mortgage these days, he said it's best to opt for the longer term and make extra mortgage payments. That way, if times get tough and you have to make cutbacks, you could be facing a $1,200 monthly note instead of $1,900.

"In this day and age you just don't know what's going to happen tomorrow. You could lose your job. I'd rather you be in a 30-year mortgage and make an extra payment or two per year than to be locked into the high payments of a 15-year mortgage. It will give you a plan B to fall back on if you lose your job," said Koos.

Bills.com president Ethan Ewing suggests that if you plan to make an extra mortgage payment or two, make them at the beginning of the year. This will allow the interest to accrue at a lower balance, saving you even more.

Stay in your home a long time

If you do decide that buying a home is the right choice for you and you do everything right, you should also stay in it as long as possible. This is assuming that there are no extenuating circumstances such as having to move for your job or needing a larger home because you have another child on the way.

You lose a lot of money in transaction costs when you sell and then buy another home

Moving and upgrading is okay, but it should be a rare occurrence—something you do maybe two, possibly three times in your life. If your salary isn't growing tremendously and you're buying a new home every seven years, you're likely causing unforeseen financial problems for yourself. Here's how: Every time you buy and sell a home, you incur massive transaction costs. Since you're mainly paying interest in the early years of your mortgage, you don't accumulate any equity in the home. When you keep doing this every seven years, you're throwing away a lot of money. And since the overwhelming majority of people buy a new home because they're upgrading, they're almost always adding to the amount of debt they owe. That bigger home also comes with bigger maintenance costs, higher insurance premiums and higher property taxes.

Let's say you buy a $250,000 home with 20 percent down on a 30-year mortgage at 4.5 percent and have closing costs of $3,500. So you put down $50,000 and pay another $3,500 in cash for the closing costs. Now let's say that your property taxes, insurance and maintenance average 4 percent of the purchase price per year. And—though this is highly unlikely given the recent real estate market, but we'll give it to you anyway—let's assume 3 percent annual appreciation on your home. Given that situation, you'll be paying $1,013 for your principal and interest and roughly another $1,000 per month for homeowners insurance, flood insurance, property taxes and maintenance. That brings your total monthly living expense to $2,013. If you want to keep that within

25 percent of your gross income, that means you had better be bringing home about $96,000 per year.

You're likely increasing your mortgage debt when you upgrade

Now, let's say that five years later you want to move and upgrade to a home that costs $315,000. You didn't get a big promotion or inherit some money, you just decided you wanted a bigger and better house with a larger kitchen for entertaining and a nice man cave downstairs (and you're tired of seeing all this nice stuff that you don't have on HGTV). With the 3 percent price appreciation, your current home is now worth about $290,000. You put it on the market and it doesn't move, so you eventually have to settle for $280,000. They you have to pay the realtor his or her 6 percent commission, which leaves you with $263,200 from the proceeds of the sale of your home. At the end of year five, you will still owe $182,316 on your old mortgage. So after you pay that off you're left with $80,844 to put down on your new home.

You buy the $315,000 home, roll all the entire $80,844 over as a down payment, then pay cash for the $4,000 in closing costs. Your total monthly living expense is now $2,236. When you consider that you're only spending $223 more per month for such a bigger house, it doesn't seem like that big of a deal.

The problem is that you now have a $234,156 mortgage instead of the $200,000 mortgage you started with five years ago. And since you had $182,316 on your mortgage when you sold your house, you just dug yourself $51,840 further into debt. Extrapolating that over the course of 30 years (assuming you actually stayed in the house and rode the mortgage out until the end), you'll have paid $42,720 in interest on that added debt. You also spent $20,800 simply on transaction costs ($16,800 for the realtor's commission and $4,000 in closing costs on the new house). That is money that simply vanished into thin air. And all this assumes 3 percent appreciation (probably not realistic) and that you can actually sell the home for near your asking cost.

Buy a home, then aim to pay it off

Get the picture? It's not bad if you decide to move once every 15 years, but when you're doing this every five to seven years you're going to rapidly erode your wealth. You're going to make realtors rich off the commissions and banks rich off the interest and closing costs, but you're not going to be getting much out of it. You might have been able to squeak by like this during the years of the housing boom, but we know that was artificially inflated—and horse crap.

Jeremy Vohwinkle says that staying in a home you can live with and *need* rather than always trying to upgrade to the one you *want* can go a long way in ensuring your financial stability. Once you let emotion take over, you're more inclined to buy a bigger house than you can really afford. Or you may buy a house that will take away from other financial aspects of your life like saving for retirement or your children's education. Vohwinkle said the biggest problem is that people often upgrade to bigger homes without factoring in the increased insurance, property taxes and maintenance costs.

"People often have this desire to get a bigger and better house, no matter what kind of house they're in. And often the house they want is more than they can afford," he said.

Ideally, you want to stay in a home as long as you can, pay it off and not have to owe the bank anything. You should buy a new home or upgrade only when you can do so by maintaining the same monthly payment and by somehow adding no additional debt—and preferably less debt. You should also have a damn good reason for buying a new home, not because simply because it makes you feel good and it's your "dream" home.

You don't want to have a mortgage when you retire

Another problem is that your constant moving could come back to haunt you when you're nearing retirement. Whatever your retirement goals are when you reach your golden years, you should ideally want to have your home paid off and not be paying a mortgage every month. But when you're upgrading and buying a new house every ten years, that's hard to do because you're constantly adding to your debt and resetting your mortgage. Say you start with a 30-year mortgage when you buy your first home at age 32, then you buy a new home with a new 30-year mortgage when you're 43, then you do it again when you're 56. Now you're four years from when you said you wanted to retire and you have 26 years left on your mortgage. Had you just stayed put or maintained your mortgage level, you would have only four years left and would likely be able to pay it out in cash.

Back in the day, people bought homes, lived in them most of their lives and worked to pay them off. That's how they did shit back then. They didn't have as many foreclosures, they had more money in the bank and less of their lives were leveraged by mortgage debt.

"These days people are house-hopping; they're always looking to upgrade. But they always take on new debt or dump so much money into their house," says Vohwinkle. "It's a different mindset than our grandparents used to have. They bought a house, would live in it for decades, then pay it off before they retired."

Save big by refinancing

If you're following any of this advice already, you have a 30-year fixed mortgage and you plan to live in your home for quite a while. Interest rates are always on the move, and there's no telling where they will be 5 years, 10 years or 20 years from now. The good thing about a fixed-rate mortgage is that it never matters where interest rates head because you'll always be paying the same rate as the day you signed the mortgage. Your property taxes and insurance can certainly increase, but if you have a fixed-rate mortgage and you're paying $800 per month for principal and interest, that's what you'll still be paying for principal and interest in 2030.

Check when the savings on the new loan will recoup the closing costs

It's hard to beat a fixed-rate mortgage, but when interest rates decline and you have the opportunity to shed a couple of percentage points, you should certainly consider it. Knowing when to refinance should be left to a few good mathematical formulas. Refinancing often involves a few thousand dollars in fees, so you have to make the decision carefully. You have to make sure that you'll make back those fees in savings within a couple of years.

Andrew Schrage, editor at Moneycrashers.com, says that it's usually not worth it to refinance when you're looking at a half percent or less. Use an online calculator like the ones at Interest.com to see how much you'll save by refinancing. While you might be excited at the prospect of saving $200 per month, you'll be shocked to see how much that can add up over time. Dropping two points on a $300,000 mortgage could easily save you more than $100,000 over the course of the loan.

"If you have a 6 percent mortgage and can get it down to 4 percent, you're going to save a lot on your mortgage payment," says Schrage. "While you might be paying back the closing costs for a couple of years, it's eventually going to put a lot of money back in your pocket."

Your house is not that great of an investment

As of November 2011, the median U.S. house price stood at $164,500, a whopping 28 percent down from its peak in 2006. Never before has the phrase "real estate only goes up" sounded like such a line of BS.

This "investment" has high maintenance and carrying costs

Forget everything you heard. You really shouldn't consider your house an investment. At best, it's a crappy one. Yes, ordinarily a house's value will rise over time, but houses have serious expenses that will drain money from your wallet faster than a teenager. "A house is a liability, not an investment, unless the cost of owning is less than the cost of renting. Even then, there are property taxes, maintenance and insurance on the structure forever," says Killelea.

The point is you have to pay money on a monthly basis simply to own this "investment."

Big gains on real estate over time are smaller than they appear

It's hard to picture this when you see your parents bought their house 30 years ago for $40,000, just paid it off and it's now worth $250,000. A $210,000 profit sounds pretty darn good until you take a very close look at it.

First of all, let's say they bought that house with 20 percent down and a 30-year fixed rate mortgage. Back in 1980, interest rates ran a whopping 12 percent. Over the course of 30 years they likely would have refinanced a coupe of times to lower rates, so for argument's sake, let's say that over the course of that time, they averaged 7.5 percent on their mortgage. Assuming they didn't just pay off the mortgage early they would have paid over $48,000 in interest over those thirty years.

Now assume that they spent an average of 3 percent per year on maintenance and upkeep. That's another $36,000 over those thirty years. Property taxes are typically 1.25 percent of the purchase price. That's another $15,000. And then there is insurance, which could have easily averaged out to 1.5 percent over the years, for a total of $18,000.

This adds up to more than $157,000 that they've spent over the years on that $40,000 house. If it's now worth $250,000 and they could actually sell it for that amount, that would net them a $93,000 profit. That's no small chunk of change, but it's far from the $210,000 profit you'd initially thought. And in all that time it's highly unlikely that they didn't remodel once or twice, add a room or a carport, or throw in another $10,000 to $20,000 in upgrades. If you take the max route on that, they've only made a $73,000 profit on the house.

Then factor in inflation over the years, and the return is not all that impressive.

Think about opportunity cost and other investments you could make

You also have to think of "investments" in terms of options and opportunity cost. Had they invested their $8,000 down payment in the stock market instead and earned the 9 percent historical average, they would have netted a profit of $106,000. The downside is that they'd likely have to pay large capital gains taxes on that.

"I was never taught that a home was an investment. It's a place to keep you safe from the elements and a warm place to raise a family. It's not an investment and has never been," says Kimberley Foss.

Depending on how you look at it, a house *may* qualify as an investment. It's just dangerous to let that be your ultimate reason for acting on a home. And it's a fairly poor investment at that when compared to stocks.

Consider that:

- A house will not provide you a single dollar of positive cash flow until you sell it—if you can sell it. Many stocks pay quarterly dividends.
- You have to pay insurance, taxes and maintenance for your house. A stock portfolio costs you nothing more than a hundred dollars or so a year in transaction and trading fees.
- The only way to get money from your house is to sell it or borrow against it with a HELOC or home equity loan.

You risk becoming house poor

The biggest danger in viewing your house as an investment is that you may be tempted to dump all of your money into it. You maximize your lending capacity and buy the biggest house you can. You take out home equity loans and upgrade bathrooms with new slate tile floors. You get a new kitchen with top-of-the-line appliances. You have landscape companies plant towering palm trees in your front yard. You add a $4,000 high-tech solar-powered hot-water heater. And you do it all because you feel that your house is such a great investment it's all going to pay off later.

Say a person buys a $200,000 house, makes $60,000 in renovations and improvements over two years, and thinks they're going to sell it for $300,000 like they saw someone did on HGTV. Unfortunately they have no control over the housing market, and if they buy into the old adage that "real estate only goes up," they've missed the news for the past few years.

And, just because they put $60,000 in their home doesn't mean their home is worth $60,000 more. It's only worth what people are willing to pay for it. This depends on the value of other homes in their neighborhood, outside economic forces and when they plan to sell. Also, the longer a person holds onto their home after a remodeling project, the less likely they are to recoup its value because design tastes can change over time. Even in a good market, that $60,000 in improvements might only be worth $30,000 to $40,000 come sale time. That still puts them at a loss of $20,000 to $30,000 on those improvements.

According to Smart Money, kitchen improvements are worth the most in terms of resale value. Even so, they typically recoup only 70–80 percent of their costs. That means a $20,000 kitchen remodel might be worth only $14,000 to $16,000 when it comes time to sell the house. That may be worth it if it helps for a quick sale but you've still lost a few thousand dollars or, at the very best, broken even. Green updates, such as efficient windows, a new roof and insulation, typically only recover 65 percent of their costs. And some improvements, such as adding a swimming pool, are largely agreed to have no resale value at all. In fact, having a pool detracts from a home's appeal to buyers these days.

Buy a house to live in it

The bottom line is that while all of these improvements might make your home a lot nicer place to live, they should never be considered "investments." Many of these things may increase your home's market value, but it's not a dollar-for-dollar increase. You might dump $50,000 into your $200,000 home that you want to sell, and two weeks later it is appraised for $235,000. Two months after that, you finally find a buyer—and they offer you $230,000. Congratulations on selling your home...and on losing $20,000.

That's not to say you shouldn't improve and upgrade your home. Remodel your kitchen, build a deck, redo your bathroom, replace your old single-pane windows. But do it because you want to make your home more comfortable. Do it because it makes your home a nicer place to live. Do it because you enjoy it. Not because you're looking for a place to "invest" your money.

The one thing that a house does have going for it as an investment is that you can live in it. You can't live in your stock portfolio, nor will it won't keep you warm at night and out of the rain. If the time is right for you to buy a house, do so, but not because you think it's an investment that's going to make you money.

Do the math when chasing energy efficiency

Energy efficiency is big business these days. Not just because it is "green" and helps the environment, but because it saves you money. Or so that's what they want you to believe. That's not to say that all reputedly energy-efficient appliances are a waste but many of them do not always pay for themselves.

Are the savings worth the cost?

Energy-efficient appliances don't always pay off. You should weigh the cost and benefits of new appliances carefully before making a purchase. You may save some money by replacing your 22-year-old refrigerator, but junking a 7-year-old dishwasher that works perfectly may not save you enough to make the new purchase worthwhile. The average U.S. household spends approximately $2,200 per year on energy—nearly half of which goes to heating and cooling, according to Energy Star and the Lawrence Berkeley National Laboratory. Of the rest, about 14 percent goes to heating water, 12 percent to lighting and only 13 percent to appliances such as refrigerators, washing machines, dryers and dishwashers. So spending a lot of money to save on that 13 percent may not always add up.

Focus on heating and cooling; all the other stuff is peanuts. Spending an extra $600 on an "efficient" refrigerator that will save you $18 per year means it will take you 30 years to recover the cost. By that time you'll likely have bought another refrigerator.

Look at the payback period

You should always start by looking at the payoff period on how long it will take to recover the extra money you're spending. So how do you calculate that?

It's simple. Take the cost of the most efficient appliance, and subtract from it the cost of the least efficient appliance. This gives you a price difference. Then, if you can, compare the Energy Star labels and find out the annual savings the higher-efficiency product will produce annually.

Now, take the price difference and divide it by the annual cost savings. This tells you how many years it will take to recoup the extra money you're spending. Five years? Go for it. Twenty-eight years? You might think twice about being green. It's especially important to think about it if you plan on moving in ten years.

And then there are other products like windows, insulation and doors. These can make an impact on your energy consumption, but do the math before making a move just because a salesman or someone on HGTV said it would save you money. You might be surprised at what you find.

.

CHAPTER 2

STUFF ABOUT YOUR CASH

As they say, cash is king.

Cash puts a roof over our head, it gives us food to eat, it keeps us warm in the winter, it can protect us in times of danger and it can show us a damn good time. When we're young, our parents send us to school so we can learn to read and get a decent education so that we can go to college and someday get a good job. And the whole reason for doing that is so that we can earn *cash*. And we work for cash because you need it to live.

Cash comes to us via direct deposit, a check or a wire transfer. Money pulled from our checking accounts, our savings account, the safes in our closets is all cash. It can be earned, received as a gift, given away, even stolen. We can spend it, waste it, blow it, save it, invest it and even burn it.

The interesting part is that while we're so obsessed with cash, cash is drastically changing its shape. We're slowly moving towards a "cashless" society. Checks are rapidly giving way to electronic payments and debit cards are quickly taking the place of the greenbacks in your wallet. A 2010 survey by comScore, Inc., found that over 60 percent of Americans use online bill paying, and according to the Nilson Report, American consumers spent $1.39 trillion via their debit cards that same year.

Mobile payments are already in operation in some markets; before long we may be walking around with nothing but our cell phones. Someday, your phone may serve as your entire wallet, carrying your I.D. and credit and debit card information. And at that point, your bills and coins will be back at home in a collector's box. The "cash" of the future may be nothing more than a constantly-changing number on the screen of your laptop or smart phone.

Your "cash flow" is how it comes in and goes out. When you get paid, how much your paycheck is, when and how much you pay on your mortgage, your utility bill, your car loan and your insurance are all part of your cash flow. Any time you spend or receive money affects your cash flow. It's important to learn how to effectively manage your cash flow; you optimally always want to have more money coming in than you have going out.

"Make sure what you have going out matches what you have coming in. Hell, you want to have less going out," says Bill Hammer. "It's a simple concept, but many people don't understand it. You need to look at your cash flow over the course of months."

For some people, all you know is that they get paid every two weeks, their mortgage or rent is due on the first, their cable bill is due on the 3rd, their utility bill and car note is due on the 10th. Maybe they pay all the other bills as they come in. If they feel they're doing well enough—meaning they always have money to pay the bills—they may not pay much more attention beyond that. They might figure that since they're not in the hole every month and always have the funds to cover the bills, everything must be fine.

While you may be doing better than some people, everyone can benefit by paying a little more attention to their cash flow. You're going to need a budget, and you're going to need the right bank accounts and the right allocation in those bank accounts. Think of the budget as a roadmap that can help you get where you want to go. Tracking these things lets you take a closer look at your spending to see where your money is going. It gives you the ability to cut some of the fat and frivolous spending out of your budget. Schoolteacher and author of the book *How to Survive (and Perhaps Thrive) on a Teacher's Salary* Danny Kofke says having a spending plan in place is the backbone of financial security.

"You should know how much you are spending. People just don't pay attention to it, and it's why so many are in trouble. Know what you need to live on a weekly basis and what you need to pay your bills every month," says Kofke.

You also should understand the term "liquidity." It is basically a measure of how readily an asset can be converted into cash. Cash itself, in the form of paper money or on a debit card, is the most liquid of assets. You can use it immediately and can spend it on the drop of a hat if you need to for necessities or for fun.

One of the most illiquid assets you can own is real estate. Owing a home isn't a bad thing, but owning a $300,000 home and only having $7,000 in the bank means you have a serious liquidity problem. The problem with banking your worth in real estate is that it cannot be turned to cash very easily. If you ran into a problem and needed an extra $10,000, you'd have to either sell your house or borrow against its equity (if you have any) with a home equity loan or line of credit. With the latter you're going to pay interest charges and incur a new debt that you could be paying off for years. And as for selling your home, do you really want to have to think about that every time you come into some big unexpected bill? Even if you were willing to pack up, move and do just that, you still have the hassle of trying to sell your home and then having to take a 7 percent loss on the realtor commission.

In general, you should aim to have a fair amount of liquidity because it gives you financial strength. You'll see many people that have nice homes and plenty of toys and luxuries, yet they barely have any money to handle everyday expenses, let alone emergencies.

On the other hand, you don't want to stay too liquid. Total liquidity would mean having no house, no car, no investments or retirement account—just a big, massive pile of cash in your home. The problem with that is that due to inflation alone, you're already losing 3 percent a year on your money. The $30,000 a person has stashed in their basement will only be worth about $29,100 next year. And the year after that it will really only be worth about $28,227.

"You're going to have to do something to beat 3 percent over time, because if not you're actually going to be losing money by doing nothing. Do something with that money to maintain and hopefully increase your purchasing power," says Hammer.

Even if you don't go to that extreme but still keep all of your money in your savings or checking account, as many people do, you're still could be losing out—not only because of inflation, but also on the gains you could be making on that money. And you really need to think about inflation because it's going to continuously eat away at your money. Adam Koos, president of Libertas Wealth Management, believes that due to the way the U.S. government has been printing new money lately, inflation will be a serious concern in coming years.

"Everything we buy from our cars to our gas to our food to our cell phones to our computers is going to go up dramatically in price," says Koos. "For me it's not a question of if, but when. Not earning anything on your money and having excess liquidity is dangerous."

That's why it's smart to *invest* a reasonable portion of your money. When you do invest money, such as in CDs, bonds or stocks, you'll be giving up some of that liquidity—but you'll be getting paid to do so. Instead of earning .05 percent on your money, you could be earning 2 percent, 5 percent, 9 percent or more over time.

Generally, the longer you're willing to do without your money, the more you can earn. Put your cash in a money market account, where you can withdraw it at any time, and you'll be lucky to earn half a percent on it. Put your cash in a 1-year CD and you might earn 1.5 percent on it. Put it in an I Bond, where you have to hold it for five years to cash it penalty-free, and you might be able to earn more than 3 percent. Buy stock in a solid blue chip company, hold onto it for 30 years, and you may very well earn 10 percent or more over time if you earn and reinvest dividends.

Whatever you do, always manage your cash properly and always try to earn a return on it, even if that's a measly half percent.

Get organized

To have any kind of decent financial life, you have to stay organized. It's hard for a person to pay bills and know what's coming in and what's going out when they don't even know what's going on or can't find the things they need.

Organization saves you money and prevents some financial mistakes

Chris DeBarres is co-owner of Help Unlimited, Inc., a day-to-day money management company that helps people get their financial lives in order. He says that disorganization can cause many financial headaches and problems. Piles of bills and papers haphazardly stacked on tables and desks and on the floor often result in late payments, missed payments and a plethora of other problems. If you live like that you're less likely to know the balance in your bank accounts, how much you owe on your credit cards and when your utility bill is due. The big problem is that a mess like this ultimately causes you to lose money.

"If you are not organized with your personal finances, chances are you are throwing away money," says DeBarres. "It's easier to miss payments, and you'll be incurring late fees and interest charges. And if you're going along not reading your bills, you could be missing things."

Phone companies, credit card businesses and subscription services can be notorious for slipping new charges on your bills. If you don't read them, you're never going to notice. DeBarres says there is no right or wrong way to get organized, but in general you should have a file cabinet or box for paper statements and a folder on your computer for digital statements.

Organize with apps

There are also many apps available for the iPhone and Android that can help you get your financial life in better order. They're great because they're easy to use and they let you access your finances wherever you are, so you don't have to rely on a stack of papers or folders. A few good apps to consider include Accounts, Ace Budget and Home Budget; all can help you track your account balances, income, and expenses and provide detailed charts and graphs about your finances. But keep in mind that if you're going to use apps to track your finances, you should institute some security measures like a password for your phone and be sure to back up the data regularly to a website or a laptop.

Track your everyday cash flow

You should have a good picture of your own cash flow because it can affect everything from your savings and your debt to your ability to pay your bills. Cash flow is not just about receiving and spending money but about *when* you spend it and receive it—the paycheck you get every two weeks, the mortgage you pay every month, the money you spend on utilities, the money you send to your insurance company, and all the other monthly bills you pay.

"Cash flow is the most important element of your financial well-being," says Pitzl. "It doesn't matter how much money you invest, how much you save in taxes or how much you make; if you overspend, all of those things become irrelevant."

Think about your small everyday purchases

While it might take only a few minutes to sit down and add up the big bills you pay every month, most of us don't track what happens with our money on a daily basis. That's because it can be so difficult to add up all the small purchases: the $5 for the coffee and the bagel at Starbucks, the $11 to top off the gas tank, the $10 for the DVD you picked up at the register, the $4 for the combo meal at the fast food joint when you were headed home late one night. This is the kind of stuff that we don't always factor in when we're thinking about how much we're spending every month.

If you're a hefty debit card user and can add up and organize all these purchases on your monthly statement, then do it. Track it for a few months, organize the spending by category, and you might be surprised at just how much you're spending on a daily and weekly basis.

Stick to cash if you spend too much with your debit card

Adam Koos recommends switching strictly to cash if you have a lot of trouble tracking your purchases when you're using a debit card. As opposed to a debit card where you just swipe and buy things, there is something about holding cold, hard cash in your hands that really hits home for a lot of people. You're likely inclined to think more about your purchases when you use cash than you do when you use plastic. A $65 pair of jeans, $5 latte and $32 lunch is going to seem that much more expensive when a person pays with cash.

"It's just too easy for money to slip through your hands, and you never even know where it has gone by the end of the month. If you pay with cash, you're going to think a lot harder about it," says Koos.

Create separate accounts for separate goals

Some people lump all of their liquid assets into a checking account and a savings account. That's fine and dandy if you're just paying a few bills, but you may find it easier to track and visualize your financial goals if you open multiple savings accounts for multiple goals. Since it's usually free to open a savings account at a trusted online bank, there's no reason not to open a few so long as you can keep track of them. Hammer says it's a good idea provided you keep an eye on the fees and don't go overboard; it's okay to have three or four savings accounts for separate goals, but you really don't need ten.

Open multiple accounts

Saving for a new car? Good, open an account just for that. Saving for a down payment on a home? A trip to Africa? You can have accounts for those as well.

You'll be able to link these accounts straight to your primary checking account that you can use to fund your savings account or withdraw from. Using a number of accounts like these allows you to compartmentalize and divide your money into "virtual" piles for different purposes, just like you did when you were a kid. This way, you can visualize your goals. Hammer says the most important thing is that when you combine a dedicated account with an identifiable monetary goal, it makes it much easier to track your progress on attaining that goal.

"If you throw [your money] all together it can be hard to see what is what. It can be easier to track when you have different accounts for different goals," he says.

And there's no problem with starting small. If you're saving for a trip that is going to cost you $2,000, set aside an account for that, then break it down into small chunks. That's only $175 per month (or $43 per week) that you have to set aside for the next year. Make a commitment to do it, set up the link between the two accounts, and make it a habit to make a transfer every week.

Divide every paycheck

There are times early in your adult life when you might be living paycheck to paycheck. Unfortunately, that's a stark reality for many Americans. But if you learn to cut your budget in some places, you'll eventually have a little money left over. And when you do, you might find it easier to divide every paycheck on the spot. With today's online banking capabilities, you should have multiple accounts opened that all tie to your checking account.

Different accounts for different purposes

Once your paycheck hits your main checking account, divide it up between the accounts you should be focusing on. Your main distributions should be: 10 percent to your savings account; 10 percent to a supplemental IRA (or 20 percent to your IRA if you don't have a retirement plan at work); 10 percent to your emergency fund. Beyond that you can make other allocations, but don't go overboard. Instantly splitting up your paycheck the moment you get it helps you save more and prevents you from spending too much.

If your $1,500 paycheck hits your checking account and you just let it sit in there, you're more likely to spend it. If you're aiming to save 20 percent of every check, then make the transfer that day; otherwise you may very well spend that $300 before you know it. Another option is to have your paycheck sent directly to your main savings account, then disperse the funds from there.

It helps prioritize your spending

Dividing your paycheck also helps you resist the temptation to spend more money than you should be during the month. For instance, if you need roughly $2,000 per month to pay all of your bills and you're making $2,900 per month after taxes, then have each $1,450 paycheck sent to your savings account. Then, on each payday after the funds have landed in your account, you can transfer $1,000 to your checking account. Making your savings account your default account and putting only what you need in your checking can help you spend less money. When you need extra funds to make a purchase outside of your normal necessities, you'll have to dip into that savings account, making you think twice about what you're buying.

Michael Friedman is a management consultant and creator of the economics blog The Economist. He says that "enveloping" funds—earmarking them for different specific purposes—from each paycheck helps you learn where your money needs to be going and creates a mindset of automatic saving. "It teaches the person the idea of the scarcity of their funds. It teaches them that if they're going to spend more money than they have allocated for one thing, they're going to have to take it away from money that they have allocated for another thing," says Friedman.

Always think about opportunity cost

Opportunity cost is the cost of an activity that is measured in terms of the value of another alternative that is not chosen. In terms of your personal finance, it means taking a look at what else you could have done with money that you spent on something or put somewhere else. Understanding the concept of opportunity cost and thinking about it when making financial decisions helps you keep your financial priorities and goals in clear view.

What else could you do with the money you're going to spend?

For instance, let's say that you were shopping for a new car and were stuck between a $22,000 vehicle and a $26,000 vehicle. We're going to assume that the first vehicle meets all of your needs, but the second vehicle looks a lot cooler and has a few more amenities that you would like to have. The opportunity cost is that $4,000 and what else you could do with that money. You could use that $4,000 to pay down some debt, boost your IRA contribution or pad your emergency fund. If you were to put that $4,000 away in your Roth IRA and earned an 8 percent return on it over the next 20 years, you'd have over $18,000. Now think about that $4,000. It may be only $4,000 today, but in twenty years that could be an extra $18,000 in your hands. In that case, the opportunity cost of the price difference in that vehicle is a whopping $18,000. Is it worth it now?

Looking at all purchases in terms of opportunity costs will help you better weigh your decisions. Often it will help you both cut back on frivolous spending and save more money. If you're spending $100 per month on a gym membership and you go there only two or three times per month, is it really worth it? Could you get your workout in at home with some dumbbells or at the outdoor exercise equipment on the park? If so, and you banked that $100 per month, just think of how much additional savings it would give you over the years.

Get more for your money by avoiding too much luxury

You can also think of opportunity cost not just in terms of saving and paying down debt but in terms of maximizing your discretionary purchases. Would you rather have a very nice night out for $150 or three fun nights out for $50 each? In the latter case you're not saving any money, but you're maximizing your entertainment value. You should also think about opportunity cost when it comes to name-brand merchandise; often you could get two or three pieces of non-name-brand clothing for the price of one "luxury" product.

You don't have to give up having fun or getting the merchandise you want, just learn how to do it more cheaply. Making smarter purchasing decisions will maximize the value of your dollar. Then when you're out buying, you'll be thinking about the opportunity of what you could do with that extra money you're not spending.

Conscious spending

J.D. Roth, editor of Getrichslowly.org, says you should also think about opportunity cost in something he calls "conscious spending." It's basically about using your discretionary income to buy the things you really need first before you buy all the other stuff you *think* you need. This, of course, assumes that you're already taking care of your financial obligations like saving for retirement, paying down debt and having an adequate emergency fund in place. Once you do that, if you prioritize spending your discretionary income on hobbies and interests you truly like instead of on buying things just for the hell of it, you're going to find it much more pleasurable to live within your means.

"So many times we get wrapped up in spending on all of these things we think we're supposed to buy instead of doing the things we like," says Roth. "The less of your income you can live on, the more you'll have to spend on the things you enjoy in life."

Maximize the return on your cash

Always think in terms of how much your money is earning. Interest rates suck nowadays, but there's no point in not trying to milk every penny you can out of the money you have. Passive income, even if that's only $100 a year, is better than no income. That's because you don't have to do a damn thing to earn it.

Interest-bearing savings accounts and CDs

Start with your savings and emergency savings accounts. Find an online bank that offers the highest rates, and park your money there. Just make sure it's FDIC-insured.

Then there are CDs (certificates of deposit). If you're scared to lock up too much money in a long-term CD, consider "laddering." Laddering CDs is buying a series of CDs with incremental maturity dates. For instance, a person might invest $5,000 by buying five CDs with maturity dates every six months. Each CD acts as a rung on the ladder and as each CD matures, the money is reinvested in a long-term CD, typically for five years. The proceeds are then reinvested into more long-term CDs, but as each maturity date arrives, the holder of the CD ladder has the opportunity to put those funds into higher-yielding CDs or access the cash penalty-free if need be.

The problem with CDs is that as of the time of this writing, their interest rates are unimpressive—if you're lucky you might be able to get 2 percent. Another similar option is to put some funds in bonds, though you're going to have to sit on them for a year or more if you want to walk away with your money.

High-dividend-paying stocks

Another option is to consider stock in some of the solid companies paying high dividends. If CDs were paying 5 percent, it wouldn't be advisable to put short-term cash in the stock market, but with interest rates this pathetic, it might be your best option.

The dividend yield is the total amount paid each year in cash dividends divided by the current price of the shares. It's the income-generating potential of a company, much like the interest you earn from a CD. The drawback is that the money you put in stock isn't FDIC-insured like that in a bank. In other words, putting your money in the stock market is a risk—you can lose money.

But you can minimize the risk, and your anxiety, by considering the beta value of the shares before you buy. Beta value is a common measurement of how volatile a stock is compared to the overall market. A beta below 1 means a stock's price moves less than the market average, while anything above 1 means the stock moves more than the market. So the smartest place to put your money is in companies that have a long record of paying substantial dividends AND a beta lower than 1.

These companies are not hard to find. Some of the more notable blue chip stocks in the Dow Jones include Verizon, Coca-Cola Co., ExxonMobil Corp., AT&T, Merck, Pfizer, Intel and Proctor and Gamble. As of the time of writing, Verizon was paying a whopping 5.65 percent dividend yield.

Investing in shares with high dividend yields also provides some protection against falling share prices. Let's say you invested in Verizon and the stock price fell 2 percent over the next year. You'd still come out ahead because of the 5.6 percent dividend you were paid. And you'd still beat the return on any CD you could get.

And even if those shares do decline in value, you don't actually lose money until you sell them and "lock in" your losses. If you decided to invest in dividend-paying stocks to try to earn a little more on your cash, you likely won't have to lock up your principal for 30 years, but you should expect to hold on to these shares for at least the next few years. So don't even consider putting money in stocks that you'll need access to in the next year. You could have a stroke of luck, earn some dividends and see the stock rise a few percentage points in the next few months, but you could also lose principal.

With the Federal Reserve determined to keep interest rates at record lows until at least mid-2013, it will be at least that long before CDs or money market accounts are paying competitive returns again.

Pay your bills...on time

According to the 2009 Consumer Financial Literacy Survey by the National Foundation for Credit Counseling, nearly 34 million Americans admit they have been late on credit card payments. Another 18 million said they missed payments entirely. Nearly 26 percent of respondents admitted that they do not pay all of their bills on time.

Late fees can really add up

It sounds simple, but paying your bills on time really can save you a lot of money over the course of your life. When you're late on a bill you're not only hit with a late payment, you could possibly see a ding in your credit score too. Late fees can add up to $25 for credit cards, 5 percent for your phone bills, up to $8 for cable bills, and even more for utility bills. Then there's the car note and mortgage, where a late fee could be as steep as $50.

And don't even think about being late on the rent. Many landlords hit tenants with late fees of up to $100, and the longer it goes the worse it gets. My wife works in the apartment industry and used to tell me about tenants who would consistently be late on their rent month after month. They would drag it on so long every month that they would dramatically increase how much they owed the complex. Let's say the $800 rent was due on the first of the month. By the 4th of the month, there were assessed a $50 late fee. If by the tenth of the month the property has still not received the rent, it would file eviction, when means paying a clerk fee and a constable fee that can add up to $150 or more. There were actually tenants who did this every month, essentially increasing their rent from $800 to $950 simply because they didn't pay on time.

Being late on all of your bills could easily add up to $100 or more over the course of a month. That's $1,200 per year! Aside from the money you're also taking the hit on your credit score, which can bite you for years to come. You payment history makes up a whopping 35 percent of your FICO score, which means that a number of late payments can severely impact your credit score. And that can affect everything from your insurance premiums and credit card interest rates to your ability to get a job or an apartment.

Avoid bank fees

As the Federal Reserve cracked down on banks with the Credit Card Act of 2009, many saw the need to replace billions in lost revenue by jacking up fees on account holders. Fees, however small they may seem, can quickly eat away at your account balance over time. When you stick money in the bank, the banks turn around and loan your money out to other people and charge interest for it. They're making money off you so there's no reason for fees.

Checking accounts should be free, or almost free

You shouldn't be paying anything for your checking account. Common fees to look out for include monthly maintenance fees ($5-$7/month at some big banks), per-check fees, starter check fees and fees for paper statements. Also be on watch for a "check image fee" that some banks like Chase stealthily slap onto your statement every month. Others want to charge you a fee simply for getting a paper statement.

Avoid ATM fees

Do what you can to minimize ATM fees. If you're one that is constantly pulling out cash from non-network ATMs, you could be hit with big, big charges. Big banks often charge $2.50 per transaction when you use another bank's ATM. Combine that with the fact that you're likely paying another $2.50 (or more) ATM charge and that's $5 in fees on one transaction. Do that once a week and you're throwing away $20 a month or $240 per year simply on fees to access your money.

Fees are likely to rise

Bank fees have been rising in recent years and are likely to continue doing so. According to a study by Bankrate.com, 76 percent of checking accounts were free in 2009. In 2011, that number was only 45 percent while ATM fees were up more than $.07 from the previous year and overdraft fees were up more than $.36. Sixty percent more non-interest accounts carried fees and balance requirements in 2011 than in 2010. Average account maintenance fees were also reported to have risen more than 85 percent from $2.49 in 2010 to $4.37 in 2011. That adds up to an extra $52 per year.

The bottom line is that this shit adds up and is likely to get worse in the coming years. In 2011, Bank of America notified its customers that in 2012 it would start charging them $5 a month simply for the privilege of using their debit cards. In total, you could easily end up throwing away $200 per year. That's money that you could do much better things with like paying down debt or putting it in savings. Keep an eye on your statement every month and move your money if you think fees are taking too big a bite out of your funds.

Aim to build passive income

Passive income is simply income that you don't have to work for. It is income that comes on a regular basis with little or no effort on your part to earn it. It can include everything from rent you receive from a rental property to royalties from a book that you wrote to dividends and interest income. No matter how little it may be, passive income kicks ass because you don't have to do anything for it. You earn passive income while you sleep, you earn it while you're working your regular job, you earn it without even thinking about it.

Make your money work for you

One of the secrets of the rich is that they usually work to build some sort of passive income that keeps the money flowing in for life. They build businesses, make the right investments and use their money in ways that it makes more money. And you don't have to be a millionaire to get some passive income—a CD generates passive income through interest, stocks generate it through dividends, and a property can generate it through rental income.

David Weliver says that building some sort of passive income is the only way for many people to move beyond living paycheck to paycheck, because at some point, you have to make your money start working for you. Even if that's just a couple hundred dollars per year in dividends and interest, it's a start because it can compound and grow over time.

"You want to earn money on your money. You want to have something coming in that you don't have to work for," says Weliver. "It's sometimes the dividing line on whether you are just going to scrape by or have a more solid financial life for yourself. It all adds up over time."

Diversify your income

Jon Pedley, vice president of product management for Bills.com, says that building any kind of passive cash flow can help add diversification to your total income. For most people, their salary or paycheck from their job is their only source of income. No matter how much that can be, the fact that it's only one source can cause a problem if you lose it overnight. If your job is all of your income, you lose 100 percent of it if you get laid off. But if your total income is comprised of 15 percent investments, 15 percent from a rental property, 10 percent from a side business and 65 percent from your day job, you'll only lose 65 percent of your income if you get laid off. That's a lot of money, granted, but with all the other income you have on the side, at least you have *something* to fall back on.

When you're just starting out in adult life and don't have a lot of capital to invest, it can be very difficult to have a large amount of passive income. That's okay. The point is that you should be *trying* to build passive income through any means possible. It should grow over time, and while it may only mean $100 a year in interest when you're in your late 20s, it should mean thousands per year in dividends and capital gains when you're in your late 30s and then tens of thousands when you're in your late 40s and 50s. Of course, most of this will be in your retirement account, but the point is you are still earning passive income.

"It's all about diversification. If you think about yourself and your career as an asset, if you get hurt, fired or laid off, everything is gone," says Pedley. "Passive income, whether that is rental income, dividends or anything else, will give you some cushion."

Another positive thing is that most passive income (such as dividends and proceeds from stock sales) is taxed at the capital gains rate. That is currently only 15 percent, which is likely lower than the rate on your earned income. Plus, you won't have to pay FICA taxes on that income. So not only will you make extra money with your passive income, you'll keep a larger percentage of it than you would from your earned income.

Take a closer look at your taxes

You might be surprised to learn that according to the Tax Policy Center, a Washington research organization, approximately 47 percent of U.S. households pay no income taxes. Either they had too low of an income or they had so many deductions and credits that they eliminated the tax they would have owed. There are so many tax credits for low- and middle-income earners now that it's possible for a family of four making as much as $50,000 to pay no income taxes.

And despite what you might hear from Occupy Wall Street, our tax system is kind of lopsided in the other way: The top 10 percent of earners (households making $366,000 or more in 2006) pay about 73 percent of the taxes collected. The bottom 40 percent actually makes a profit from the federal income tax system, meaning they get more in credits than they would owe in taxes.

FICA, federal and local taxes

Whether you pay federal income taxes or not, take a closer look at your taxes and understand what you are paying. Anyone who works pays FICA taxes. The total of your FICA taxes amounts to 15.3 percent of your income. Half of that is paid by your employer and half of that comes out of your check. If you're self-employed, you have to cover the whole 15.3 percent; 12.4 percent of that goes to Social Security, 2.9 percent to Medicare. The Payroll Tax Holiday cut the employee's Social Security portion down by 2% to 4.2% but unless extended it's only good through 2012.

In any case, you'll also pay federal income taxes and possibly state and other local taxes.

At the very least, you should understand what kind of taxes you pay because they come out of your paycheck every week. And if at the end of every year you either owe a lot of money or get a lot of money back, you may want to consider adjusting your withholdings.

If you're getting money back or owe every spring

If you're getting back a lot at the end of every year, it means you're overpaying on your taxes. In 2010, the average tax refund, for those who got one, was $2,900. Wouldn't you rather just get more money on every paycheck throughout the entire year? If you adjusted your withholdings in that case to the right balance, that's an extra $111 you could get every paycheck if you got paid every two weeks. You could be earning interest on that money instead of giving Uncle Sam an interest free loan all year long.

If you owe a lot at the end of every year, you may also be paying fines and interest that you might not be aware of. So, you might actually be able to save money if you pay your taxes in full on every check throughout the year. In this case, you'll want to decrease the number of dependents you claim so that you'll pay more taxes. You'll have more taken out of every paycheck, but that might be better than having to fork out an extra $2,300 on April 15.

In the end, it may all work out in the eyes of the IRS, but there's no reason to be paying more on every paycheck than you have to. Ask your employer for a new W-4 and check out this IRS guide on how to adjust your tax withholding.

"If you're getting back $3,000 every April, that's a lot of money you could use for your own personal cash flow and savings during the year," says Joseph Pitzl.

Look for credits and deductions that may apply to you

According to Pitzl, it helps to take an interest in your taxes because there are tax implications (usually for the better) every time you undergo a life-changing event such as marriage, the birth of a child or the buying of a home. Only by being conscious and knowledgeable of the taxes you pay can you fully take advantage of the deductions and credits that apply to you. Pitzl says that the economic demographic of most Gen Xers put them right in between the 15 percent and 20 percent tax brackets.

"You should understand where you stand with your taxes. Unless you are working with a financial planner you are kind of on your own, so you need to see what credits apply to you," he says.

There are tax credits and deductions available for just about anything, ranging from your mortgage interest and having children to saving for retirement and taking a loss on some stocks that you sold. Don't file your taxes without exploring every deduction and credit you can.

You can easily do your taxes with software

Finally, don't listen to the noise about how complicated taxes are. If you're self-employed, have some employees, own some business equipment and/or have all kinds of assets, then yes, you're going to have to wander through a maze of paperwork. But if you're like 80 percent of the people out there, a regular Joe or Jane with one job, a small investment account or two, mortgage interest and a few deductions, it's not that big of a deal. You don't need to visit a tax center or a CPA to do it.

Buy yourself one of the easy-to-use tax programs like Turbo Tax or Tax Cut. It will set you back less than $30, and if you have your papers in order and readily available, you should be able to knock out your return in an hour or two. Both of these programs will run error checks and help you find other deductions that you may have missed. This is especially helpful because if you just fill out a 1040 by hand every year, you could potentially be missing lots of deductions and paying more taxes than you have to. And here's a secret: If you do decide to bring your taxes to someone, they're likely going to use a program like this anyway. Using software also makes it easy to archive your information and carry it over to the following year, simplifying the tax-filing task even more..

Avoid gambling and lottery tickets

The lottery has often been called a "tax on the poor." A 2008 study in the Journal of Risk and Uncertainty revealed that the vast majority of lottery consumers are low-income and that 20 percent of Americans play the lottery, spending more than $60 billion per year. It found that a household with an income of under $13,000 spends up to $645 (9 percent of their total income) on lottery tickets.

It's a cycle. When a person spends a disproportionate amount of their income on the lottery, it helps keep them poor—which keeps them buying tickets. The lottery is a systematic form of exploitation, and a number of studies and reports, including this one in North Carolina, have demonstrated that poorer counties have the biggest lottery ticket sales.

Another study, commissioned by the South Carolina Education Lottery, showed that while people in households earning under $40,000 accounted for only 28 percent of the state's population, they made up 54 percent of lottery players. It has also been demonstrated that poor people play the lottery even more when times are tough.

You don't have to be in the bottom income bracket to fall victim, of course. And regardless, the odds are still against you. Spending $10 on lottery tickets every week translates to $520 per year you're throwing away to a game where you stand virtually no chance of winning. According to the Powerball's website, the odds of winning the jackpot are 1 in 195 million. Your odds of winning even just $100 are 1 in 13,644. Your overall odds of winning any prize at all are 1 in 35.

Many people play the lottery because the hype is hard to ignore, especially when the jackpots climb to record amounts. Playing the lottery also gives some people *hope*, the hope that they'll win the big jackpot and that their financial problems will go away. Lotto tickets are also cheap, and it's easy to rationalize a few bucks here and there.

But it adds up over time. That $520 per year you're spending could turn into $3,680 in five years if you funneled those funds to an account and earned 5 percent on it. And your chance of having that $3,680 wouldn't be 1 in 195 million, 1 in 13,000 or even 1 in 4. Your chances would be 1 in 1—yes, *guaranteed*—because you're saving that money for yourself rather than forking it over to some attendant in a gas station in the hope that you might be the one person out there with the winning ticket. If you continued to save that money over 10 years, it would grow to $7,700. In 20 years it would be $19,433 and in 30 years it would be $38,523. In 30 years of playing the lottery, you still wouldn't have a chance of making that kind of jackpot.

According to the book *High Stakes: The Rising Cost of America's Gambling Addiction*, Americans lost more than $92 billion gambling in 2007. In 2005, 73 million Americans visited one of the country's 1,200 casinos and card rooms and in 2010, officials in 37 states pushed for more gambling to bring in more state revenue. The reason for all of this is that gambling is a losing proposition for consumers. Sure, you might win a couple hundred bucks here and there, but what does it matter if you lose $2,000 in the process? Even if you have a fairly decent footing in the middle class, an abnormal addictive personality or a compulsion for gambling could quickly eat away at your financial security.

Hey, we're not unrealistic. Gambling might be a little fun once in a while if it means throwing a twenty in a slot machine or taking a hundred dollar bill to have some fun at the poker or blackjack table. You can't pass through Vegas or a casino and not take a shot, right? And when the Powerball hits $500 million, you might want to join in on the fun. Fine, just do it with a reasonable sum of money. Limit your trip to the casino to a hundred bucks, and limit your lottery tickets to a few per month. Set a limit and stick with it. You can still enjoy the game, the thrill that you might win—and do so in a manner that won't keep you in the poorhouse.

Stay away from payday loan, cash advance and rent-to-own stores

Payday loan, cash advance and rent-to-own stores are some of the biggest financial predators in America. They milk desperate people of the little money that they have, hit them with massive fees and interest rates and put them further into debt. It's hard to see when you're facing a serious financial crisis, but doing business with any of these places is a financial disaster.

Hopefully you'll never come to this, but at some point in your life, you may run into a cash flow problem, lose your job, or have a crisis that depletes your emergency fund and find that you're running low on options. Do whatever else you have to do—pick up a little overtime at work, borrow money from your friends or family, sell your plasma, or sweep up manure at the local farm. Just do not visit theses places.

Insane fees and interest rates

Payday loans typically come in the form of a $50-$500 short-term loan with very high interest rates. Instead of "interest rate" the industry prefers to use the term "fee." Whatever you call it, it's usually high. You might borrow $100 for 14 days and pay a $15 fee. That's an equivalent of an interest rate of 391 percent. These loans are also renewable or extendable, and if you roll it over too many times it can sink you into a deep, dark financial hole. Compounding also hits you hard. If you roll over the $115 you owe them (and many people do), you're hit with another $15 fee. Do this a few more times and within a couple of months, you could owe $160.

At Advance America, the fee for a $100 loan is $20, representing a 521.43 percent interest rate. For a $350 loan, the fee is $50, representing a 372 percent interest rate. It's sad that anyone has to resort to these places, but people sometimes fall for them because they don't require a credit check, it's easy to apply, the process takes less than 20 minutes and the money is deposited in your bank account in less than 24 hours. These places prey on the poor and financially illiterate—it's no surprise that the 10,000 payday loan places in the U.S. are usually found in poorer neighborhoods or placed where there are high concentrations of lowly paid workers.

It's addictive

Just like crack cocaine or meth, you're not likely to do this just once. It's best not to start in the first place. Things go well in that one-time emergency, and you're back next month for another loan. Before long, you're good friends with the clerk at the window and you're giving up $135 per month in fees to the place.

Save your money and buy, don't rent-to-own anything

Rent-to-own can be even worse. There is no reason to even walk into these places; if you can't swing the cost of a new couch, television or Playstation 4 then buy a used one on Craigslist. Rent-to-own establishments charge sky-high interest rates and fees built into the monthly rental payments. And if you rent indefinitely or until you reach the buy out amount, you will pay far more than you would have paid for the product had you just saved the money and bought it at Best Buy.

For a simple illustration to understand the rent-to-own scam, check out this cartoon style pamphlet from the Consumer League of New Jersey. It highlights how renting to own a $200 19" television at $12 per week can end up costing you $936 by the time you've paid it off in 78 weeks. That represents a 309 percent interest rate and means you'll have paid $736 more for the product—or almost five times its original price—than had you just saved up and bought it yourself.

Don't fall for this B.S. Just save the money to buy what you want or buy something used. In many states, rent-to-own stores now have stronger disclosure regulations, but you can be assured that you still won't have a clear picture of what you're paying for.

And if you're really in a pinch? Get a cash advance on your credit card. It may be a bad idea, too—but it's a lot better than going to a pawn shop or payday loan store.

CHAPTER 3

SAVING FOR TOMORROW

"Anything that we can do to raise personal savings is very much in the interest of this country."

—*Alan Greenspan*, former Federal Reserve Chairman

Chances are that one out four of you reading this book has no personal savings. Yes, that's right—no savings. As in nothing in the bank.

Why? Some people have no savings because they're poor. Others have no savings because their money management skills are poor. Whatever the case, it's not an enviable situation to be in.

Since 1982, the savings rate in America has fallen to pathetic levels. As of September 2011, it was a measly 3.6 percent, meaning that the average worker who makes $40,000 per year only saves $1,440 each year, less than $150 per month. And this is the *average,* meaning that half of the people out there actually save less. Whether it's due to rising prices and economic hardship or frivolous spending, conspicuous consumption and poor money management, many Americans go through each fiscal year without saving a single dollar.

Going through life without savings is like walking a tightrope or hanging off the side of a 15-story building by one hand. It's dangerous and it's only a matter of time before something happens to bring you down hard.

The reality is that not only do you need savings, you also need a specific account set aside strictly for emergencies. In that account should be six months' worth of living expenses to cover you in the event of job loss, a major health issue, a big home repair, an auto repair or anything else that can come your way. Having this financial cushion may seem like a luxury, but it's necessary.

"A lot of people may not be able to save six months of income, or it may take a long time to get there, but it should still be a goal," says Andrew Schrage, an editor at Moneycrashers.com. "You should have this in place for worst-case scenarios. You don't know what kind of emergencies you'll have in life but you can at least have some money in place to help."

This is the account you keep for when life happens—and you know it always does, sooner or later. So be as ready as you can be. As with everything else we've stressed in this book, you just need to do the best you can. If you can't put away enough to cover six months worth of bills, then shoot for three months. Of course, the more you can save the better, but putting away $150 per month is better than putting away nothing every month. Something is always better than nothing. And the mere fact that you have an emergency account will put you well ahead of half of the country.

So many Americans are in the hole and don't have money to put away because they live beyond their incomes. Your ability to save is highly dependent upon your ability to live within your means. A person who spends every dollar they make is not going to be able to save anything.

So what's the best way to start saving, even if you think you can't? Make saving a priority. You have to employ the old cliché of "pay yourself first" and make it such a priority that when you get paid you put money away for yourself before you pay your mortgage and other bills. Set yourself and your accounts up so that the minute you get a paycheck, you set aside 10 percent, 20 percent, or even more *before* you do anything else.

You should have savings before anything unexpected happens. You could lose your job, you could get in a major car accident, your hot water heater could spring a leak and flood part of your house. And when it happens, you'll want to have money in the bank to cover it.

Nancy Butler, Certified Financial Planner and founder of Above All Else, says that people need to find a *reason* to save, and until they become financially conscious or experience a disaster, it may not happen. "Many people don't have a sense of financial priorities. They just don't get it. People need to see something at the end of the line, that it's going to do something for them," says Butler.

So find a reason and start somewhere. Maybe to you, retirement is too far away and not easy to think about. Fine, then start saving for a trip to Thailand, a new car, a new 65-inch LCD television. These may not be the best uses of your money when you're on a limited budget, but the point is that you'll be saving something—you'll learn how to do it.

And it gets a lot easier to save once you get into the habit of it. After a few months you'll likely be so inspired by the growth of your savings that you'll want to save more. Believe me, it can happen. After a year or so, you'll probably find you sleep a little better knowing you have that money there for emergencies. And after a few years of saving, you'll find yourself wondering how anyone could go through life without putting away some money on the side. You'll go from feeling as if you're giving up something to realizing you're actually gaining something.

Pay Yourself First

We know. When you get paid, you usually have to pay bills. You've got to pay the rent, the utility bill, the phone bill and whatever else is in that stack of envelopes on the table. But don't forget to pay yourself. First do it when you can, and then do it regularly. Aim to always pay at least 10 percent to yourself first. So if you get a $1,500 check, sock away $150 of it before you do anything else.

The first payment should be to your savings account

It's easier to save money when you pay yourself first. If you wait until the end of the month after you've paid all of your bills, it will seem like you'll never have enough left for yourself. The point of all your hard work shouldn't just be to cover the rent and bills, it should be to accumulate some money that you *keep* for yourself. So make your savings account your first stop. Paying yourself first helps ensure that you're living within your means, and it helps you meet your savings goals.

J.D. Roth, editor of GetRichSlowly.org, says that no matter how much you make, you're going to spend too much if you don't save first. "Most people wait to see if they have a little money left over and then they save it. You're never going to save much this way. You need to make savings the first thing you do," says Roth.

Make it automatic

Paying yourself first is easiest when you don't have to think about it. Use automatic withdrawals available to you through your employer or your own bank. You'll never see that money and will learn to live without it. You'll also learn to live within your means because if you put 20 percent of your paycheck in savings before you do anything else, you'll automatically be training yourself to live on only 80 percent of your income.

And don't forget to factor in that putting a dollar away *now* gives it time to grow and earn compound interest. The sooner you put away money, the more it is worth. It underlines the fact why the more you save and the sooner you do it, the more money you'll end up with in the long run.

Make it a habit

Start saving as soon as you can, because as time goes on it gets harder and harder to save money. Joe Pitzl, Director of Financial Planning for Intelligent Financial Strategies, LLC, says that establishing sound financial habits in your 20s is easier to do than trying to break bad financial habits in your 30s or 40s. Even if you're not making much money at the time, it's a lot easier to save money when you're 26 and single than when you're in your 30s and married with a child or two. And as life goes on it can get harder and harder to save money. You may start making more, but you'll also be spending a lot more on necessities every month.

"People think they'll wait until later in life to start saving," says Pitzl. "All of a sudden you're 30 years old, getting married and now you're saving for things where you to have spend money, like a wedding, a house or a baby. Now, you don't have that discretionary cash flow to save for retirement or long-term savings."

When you start paying yourself first and doing it regularly, you'll find it will become a habit that will stick with you throughout your life.

Spend Less Than You Make

This is *the* single most important step in gaining financial independence. If you cannot live within your means, you will always be on a financial tightrope. It is not possible to save money without spending less than you make, and you can not spend more than you make without incurring debt. When a person spends more then they may, they are doubly shafting themselves: They have no savings and they are piling on debt.

Start with your home and vehicle

Bringing your spending in line with your income is not something you can do simply by cutting out a Starbucks latte or skipping a night at the movies every once in a while, no matter what lame magazine articles might tell you. You'll have to take a hard cold look at your two biggest expenses—where you live and what you drive. These two things alone can have *the* biggest impact on your financial life.

When it comes to your house and vehicles buy what you *need,* not what you *want*. You may want a BMW and a $400,000 house, but in reality you could do just fine with a Toyota and a $200,000 house. And you should make these purchasing decisions based on what your income can afford you. If you're making $50,000 per year, you should probably opt for the Toyota and modest house.

Follow these rules:

- Housing costs—everything from the monthly mortgage or rent payment to property taxes, insurance premiums and condo fees—should be 28 percent or less of your gross (pretax) income.

- Your vehicle costs—the monthly payment, insurance and maintenance costs—shouldn't total any more than 10 percent of your gross income.

So if you make $40,000 per year, that means you shouldn't be spending more than about $930 a month on housing and $330 a month on transportation.

True, that's not a lot. But you'll never have a shot at financial independence if you can't get these two big expenses under control. And here's a tip: Never let a car salesman or mortgage loan officer BS you about what you "can afford." They want you to buy the bigger house and the more expensive car because it increases their commission. They do not give a crap about your financial well being. So handle situations like that this way: If a loan officer says you can afford a $300,000 house, start looking at something in the $220,000 range. If a car salesman says you can afford a $32,000 vehicle, start looking at something in the low $20s.

If someone does it on a teacher's salary, you can too

No one knows more about living within his means than Danny Kofke. He's a special education school teacher and author of *A Simple Book of Financial Wisdom* and *How to Survive (and Perhaps Thrive) on a Teacher's Salary*. He also manages to support himself, his wife and his two daughters on a salary of no more than $40,000. But Kofke does more than just scrimp by and pay his bills. He has an emergency fund in place and also saves for their retirement and even their daughters' college education. Kofke is successful not because he's a financial Superman, but because he and his wife are committed to learning to live on what they make.

"We actually live a pretty wealthy life on our income. We have only 13 years left on our mortgage, [with] a one-year emergency fund in place," says Kofke. "We did our best to avoid debt. The small things add up but nothing compares to your home and cars. So many people say they don't have any money and they're driving brand-new cars."

Think hard about your discretionary spending

Once you tackle your home and vehicle expenses, you're going to have to look at your discretionary spending. This includes everything from eating out on the weekends to the clothes you buy, what you like to do for fun and what kind of toys you have. Life is meant to be lived, of course, but you have to be realistic with your spending and always keep an eye on where your money is going. At the end of the day there has to be money left over for savings.

Something that often stands in the way of this is that we make decisions based on how we feel. "I think money problems are 80 percent emotional. People just want to spend money they don't have. If you want something that might seem a little bit out of your reach, you're either going to have to get another job, sell some things or save for it. We only have a certain amount of money coming in," says Kofke.

Be realistic about what you can afford

There's nothing wrong with spending money on these things—*if* you can realistically afford it. But if you're living the high life on $30,000 or $40,000 per year and have no savings behind it, then it's all for nothing and won't be long before the bill comes due.

Kofke identifies the types of fun he and his family can afford by planning and budgeting. That means, first, knowing how much he needs to live every month. That will tell him how much leftover funds can go towards fun. For many people that may not be a lot, but having financial security in your life means making alternative decisions—and some sacrifices.

Living within your means is a very, very simple concept, but in a credit-happy society, no one teaches us how anymore. But you *can* do it. It doesn't matter how much you make—start spending less, and bank the difference.

Set up an automatic savings plan

One of the easiest ways to help yourself save money is to set up an automatic savings plan. Your money is automatically moved without your even seeing it, so you don't have to worry about being disciplined enough to save. Your bank can set up a link between your checking account and savings account that will make drafts from your checking and deposit it in your savings account at various intervals—once a week or once a month, whatever works best for you. If you have direct deposit through your employer you may also be able to set something up that will have them automatically deposit a percentage of your pay or a specific dollar amount into your savings account.

Small amounts from automatic savings can add up. If you get a $1,500 paycheck every two weeks and set up automatic savings of 10 percent, you'll be putting away $300 per month without even thinking about it. In five years you'll have $18,000 and in ten years you'll have $36,000. And that's without earning interest.

The best part is that in the process of building up your savings you'll also be learning to live better within your means, since you'll be living on $1,350 instead of $1,500 every paycheck. And it can't be stressed enough that leaning to live within your means is a critical part of building financial strength.

Robert Henderson, president of Lansdowne Wealth Management, LLC, says that most people have a hard time saving money. They pay bills, go on trips, go to dinner, and go shopping—and then might save whatever is left over. The problem is that most of the time, there isn't anything left over. When you set up automatic deductions from your paycheck or pay account, such as contributions to an IRA or a savings account, you'll eventually learn to live without that money.

"If you can just put those automatic deductions in place you're never going to miss that money," says Henderson.

Have an emergency fund

As mentioned previously, life happens. Cars break down, theft occurs, uninsured people hit our cars, we get sick and can't work. William Hammer, co-founder of the Hammer Wealth Institute, says that having an emergency fund in place can prevent emotional struggles from also turning into a financial struggle. While the odds of these things happening each month aren't very likely, there is a good chance at least one of them will happen sometime. And they're usually associated with an unexpected bill.

"It's not that the odds of something terrible happening are that great, it's that the hardships could be devastating if you don't have the money. The emergency fund is [for] peace of mind."

Otherwise, you'll rack up debt

If you don't have an emergency fund, where will you turn in a time of disaster? Most turn to their credit cards, which is a bad idea. Others count on their home equity line of credit as a backup plan. But that, too, comes with interest. So if you get hit with a $6,000 bill to replace your air conditioning and you dip into your home equity because you don't have a dollar in savings, you'll now have to pay interest on that. Currently, that runs about 5 percent. How long is it going to take you to pay off that HELOC balance? If you take five years to pay it, that's an extra $793 you'll have paid in interest. Not having an emergency fund just makes everything twice as hard. Instead of forking out $6,000 to replace your AC (which sucks enough on its own), you now have to go without AC for a while, pull together your credit cards or apply for a home equity, finance the AC, spend five years making monthly payments, and spend an extra $800 on the whole thing. What sounds better?

Have six months' income put away

You should aim to have at least six months of living expenses put away in your fund, and more if possible. You don't need to include the fun stuff, just the minimum you need to pay the rent, keep the lights on and put food on the table. If that's $2,000 per month, then aim to divert $12,000 to your emergency fund.

That may sound too scary and totally unrealistic. Fine. Just start small, and be consistent. If you're starting from scratch, aim to make regular contributions until you reach your goal, even if it takes ten years. Having $1,500 in your emergency fund is better than zero. Hell, having $500 is better than nothing. Just have something and do your best to build it.

If you're on your game this may sound silly but it's not for many Americans. A 2011 study by the National Bureau of Economic Research showed that 50 percent of Americans would struggle to come up with $2,000 in a pinch for an unanticipated car or home repair or medical expenses. 28 percent of those surveyed said they "certainly" wouldn't be able to cope with the bill if they had 30 days, and another 22 percent said the "probably" would not be able to cover the expense.

That's pretty scary. So do what you can to count yourself in the financially strong half of the population. Do whatever you can to have some sort of emergency fund in an easily accessible checking or savings account. It's okay to try to earn some interest, but don't lock it up in a CD, in stocks or in anything that you can't access it in a day or so without a penalty.

Remember, emergencies only

And don't be tempted to siphon money from this fund to pay for a vacation or a fancy new television. Because the day after that, you may very well find yourself in an accident or in some sort of trouble where you need those funds. Remember, it's called emergency money for a reason. Think of it as self-insurance, money you hope you'll never need. Having an emergency fund is also a bedrock principle of financial strength. Having it means when things happen, you can handle it financially.

Bank your raises

Banking your raises and living on what you already earn is another great way to build wealth. Let's say you make $40,000 annually and you get an average raise of 4 percent per year. You can't be expected to not use at least part of your raises to increase your standard of living, but if you take part of that raise and divert it to your savings or retirement fund each year, you'll dramatically increase your wealth over time.

Grow your income and your savings

Using the same example, at the end of five years you'll be making a salary of $48,666. By banking half of your raise (2 percent) every year you'll have an extra $8,666 sitting in the bank. And you'll still be pulling in the extra 2 percent to have some fun with. Of course, you'll have to struggle with inflation and increased costs of living, but learning to live on that same salary can also help you create more financial stability in your life. That further helps you live within your means, keep you out of debt and build a bigger nest egg.

William Hammer, Jr. says you should also bank bonuses. "You should try to live below the salary you have. If you're making $50,000 per year, learn to live on $45,000 per year and then bank that $3,000 bonus you might get," he says. By learning to live on what you earn (and hopefully less than what you earn) and banking the differences in your raises and bonuses, you're slowly going to build a large cash cushion over time.

Build a bigger security net

The biggest benefit of banking your raises, whether they end up in your emergency fund or your retirement account, is that you're building even more of a safety net for times of emergency. And in today's world where no job is secure, banking that little extra every week is like a supplemental form of unemployment insurance. Hammer says the more unstable your job, or the more of a risk that you could lose it someday, the more of your raises you should be banking and saving instead of spending.

"Stuff happens. You want to think about diverting some of that money to savings so you'll have some extra money sitting around and can save towards your future," says Hammer.

If you're already content with your standard of living and get a big bump in salary or a promotion, you might want to consider banking more. If you constantly bank your raises and bonuses, you can dramatically build your financial strength.

Take advantage of compounding

The power of compounding is the most important tool to harness in growing your wealth. Compounding simply means that when you earn interest on your principal, that interest starts earning interest too. Over time, compounding can turn small sums into large sums. When you make continual contributions over time and then throw in compounding, sums can grow enormously.

Money you don't have to work for

According to J.D. Roth, the opportunity to make money on your money, without having to work for it, is the best way to build your savings. The more you invest and the longer you do it, the more you are going to earn through compounding.

Take $500. If you can earn 3 percent on that per year, you'll have $515 at the end of the first year. But the following year, you're earning 3 percent not just on that $500 but also on the $15 you earned the first year. So now, instead of earning $15 in interest, you earn $15.50 in the second year. In the third year you'll earn $16.36. The amount of interest you earn every year will continue to grow.

And that's only with $500. It doesn't sound like much, but if you set aside $50 every month, you'll have $3,000 in five years. If you make a 3 percent return on that money, you'll have $3,281 at the end of the term. With 6 percent, you'll have $3,585. Get the picture? Little savings can add up over time. Wealth is built through patience, persistence and repetitive, consistent actions. Save regularly and consistently, and let it ride.

Negative compounding sucks

Another reason to understand the power of compounding is because when you have debt, it can work against you. If you make only the minimum payment on your credit cards, the credit card company charges you interest on the balance you've accumulated since your purchase date. That means you're now paying interest on your interest.

"Negative compounding can kill you. If you have a credit card that is charging 20 percent interest, the longer you sit there and don't pay off the balance, the more you are going to pay in interest," says Roth. Compound interest can build up against you quickly with credit cards because they usually have high interest rates. If you have a $1,000 credit card balance with a 20 percent APR, you'll have a balance of $1,016 the next month. On the next statement, you'll be charged interest on the $1,016 instead of the $1,000. That month's interest will work out to $17.81 instead of $16. So unless you do something to pay down more of that principal, you're just growing your debt.

With each passing billing cycle, the compounding effect dramatically increases the amount of interest you'll pay. Use compounding to build wealth, not destroy it.

Keep up with (and hopefully beat) inflation

Inflation is like a leech that eats away at your money every single day. The historical annual inflation rate in the United States is about 3.34 percent, which means that for every hundred dollars you have today, it will only be worth about $96 a year from now. This really starts to add up over time. At this annual rate, prices double—or the current value of the dollar decreases by 50 percent—every twenty years.

You will be worth less every year unless you do something about it

So, the $1,000 you have in the bank today will really only be worth about $500 twenty years from now. The nominal amount of your money won't change, but the prices of everything else around you will. Your groceries that run $75 a week now will probably cost you $150 a week twenty years from now. That means that your money is half as worth as it used to be. If you don't think this is a big and real issue, go talk to your parents about how much a burger, a pair of jeans or a can of soda cost when they were young. It likely was two to three times less expensive than it is today. And when you're their age, you might be paying two to three times what you are today.

Only when you understand inflation can you understand investing and trying to earn something on your money is so important. You should fear inflation, and you should harness that fear with action. In a perfect world our incomes would be rising to keep up with inflation, but this just doesn't seem to be playing out anymore. In 2010, surveys showed that wages averaged a growth of only 1.7 percent while the inflation rate was over 2 percent. And then there are food and gas prices, which have grown even more in recent years.

"Over time, the biggest thing young people should be concerned with is increasing their purchasing power. You have to think about what your money is going to be worth ten and twenty years from now," says Bill Hammer.

Lifestyle inflation

Joe Pitzl says that you should also account for what he calls "lifestyle inflation." This is all the latest-and-greatest that you'll feel compelled to buy as technology grows. There are so many things we "need" today that didn't even exist twenty or thirty years ago: cell phones, cable, satellite and high-speed Internet access. Then there are computers, smart phones, iPads, MP3 players, DVD players, gaming consoles and more. None of these things are necessities, but we've come to think of them as expected gadgets for a middle-class household. Back in 1980, a family might have had a couple of televisions, a VCR, an Atari and a Commodore 64. Now the "standard" tech devices really add up—which means more bills.

"We just accept that $60 to $100 per monthly cell phone bill as a part of life. Those are things that, when you look at a typical CPI index, are not accounted for," says Pitzl. "Households have been experiencing a higher inflation rate with all that stuff creeping in."

What's worse, you don't know what's coming around the corner. You don't know what kinds of bills you'll be paying in ten, twenty or thirty years. In reality, Pitzl says, all of these things add up to a much higher rate of inflation. "We add in that 3 percent inflation factor, but the reality is that in ten years it's not even going to be close to that. You need to create buffers, grow your money and prepare for some of those things so you don't derail your financial plan."

Earn 3 percent per year just to maintain the value of your money

To keep up with inflation you're going to have to earn at least 3 percent on your money. And the only way you can reliability do that over time is in the stock market or with bonds. Investing in stocks means being prepared to hang in long term (like ten years or more); if you're looking for something with a shorter term simply to keep up with inflation, consider bonds. More specifically, you should consider I Bonds. The total return on Series I Bonds is calculated by adding the inflation rate, which changes every six months, to a fixed, never-changing rate that is established when you buy each bond. Lately the interest rate has been set at 0 percent, but you're still able to earn the inflation rate, which is based on the CPI. It changes every six months but usually hovers around 3 percent or so—far higher than the miniscule 1.5 percent you'll earn on a CD. The best part yet is that with I Bonds, the minimum to invest is only $25.

You'll have to hang onto your Series I Bonds for at least a year or two to make it worthwhile. If you redeem them within the first five years, you'll forfeit the three most recent months' worth of interest. After five years, there is no early withdrawal penalty. Again, I Bonds aren't quite long-term investments to grow your wealth (you really need to look to the stock market for that), but they'll at least help you try to keep up with inflation.

There's nothing you can do to immediately fight inflation in the short term. But you should always be thinking about it; it underscores the reason why you can't have all of your money sitting in a checking account earning only .01 percent.

Track your net worth

Your net worth is simply your assets minus your liabilities—basically everything you own minus the money you owe. It's your house, your car, your investments, your retirement fund, your savings accounts, your checking account and your cash minus your mortgage, car loan, credit card debt and home equity line of credit. If everything were instantly turned to cash right now, this is how much you would be "worth."

Your financial pulse

Tracking your financial pulse gives you a good clear view of your financial health. And when you track it from month to month, year to year, you can see if you're headed in the right direction. A 2011 study from the Economic Policy Institute revealed that the median U.S. household had less wealth in 2009 than it did in 1983. In 2009 dollars, median wealth fell from $71,900 in 1983 to only $62,900 in 2009. It also found that in 2009, roughly one in four households had zero or negative net worth while 37.1 percent of house holds had a net worth of less than $12,000.

Without a doubt. there is a growing problem with the distribution of wealth in this country. But there's also the reality that nothing can be done about that at the moment. Sure, people can protest, write blog posts, raise awareness, promote higher taxes on corporations and join a political party that advocates the mass redistribution of wealth. But in the meantime, we're still going to get poorer unless we do something about it in our own lives. All of these studies, facts and figures about the upper 1 percent are useless if we can't paint a clear picture of our own finances.

Measure your progress

Whether you have a net worth of only $230 or even a negative net worth doesn't matter. You still need to track it. Your net worth is a measure of your overall financial progress, and monitoring it is a daily incentive and reminder to make the right financial decisions. If you're in line with where you should be, tracking your net worth can "help you see what kind of progress you're making and help guide your financial priorities," says Nancy Butler. "Along with a solid budget, keeping an eye on your net worth can help keep you moving in the right direction." Continuing in the right direction can build confidence as well. Even arriving at a zero net worth from a negative net worth can be a milestone.

The easiest way to track your net worth is with a spreadsheet. All you have to do is create fields for all of your assets and liabilities, and then create formulas that subtract the difference. Each month, you can plug in your balances to get an updated picture of your net worth. If this sounds daunting, there are many free net worth spreadsheets available online, including this one at CNET.com, that you can download and customize. You can also use software such as Net Worth Express or My Financial Statement.

Liquid and total net worth

When you do track your net worth, you should also be sure to look at two numbers: your total net worth (including your home) and your liquid net worth (not including your home). That's because depending on your financial situation, including your home in your net worth can give you a skewed, and perhaps too optimistic, view of your finances. If after deducting all of your liabilities you have $80,000 in home equity and $15,000 in liquid assets, that $95,000 in net worth isn't as great as it sounds. That's because the equity in your home is worth nothing until you sell the home—if you're selling it. So in reality, at this moment in time, your net worth is really only $15,000.

There are going to be months when your net worth takes a little dip. During some months you're going to have big expenses—perhaps a big home repair bill, a college tuition payment, or a down payment on a car. Or maybe the stock market takes a hit and your portfolio is down by 5 percent. This is fine. It's perfectly normal to have months where your net worth decreases slightly, but what you should see is a steady growth upward over time. That is why you want to track it over the long run.

Don't fear the stock market

The stock market hasn't been kind to many Gen Xers. There was the dot-com bubble burst of 2000, the housing crash and banking crisis of 2007-2008, and the debt crisis of August 2011. The market plunged during all of these events, costing investors trillions of dollars in losses. If you've been in the market all of these years, it's likely that in the past decade you've done little more than break even and, if you were lucky, earned a couple of percentage points. Or like many people, you may even be down—meaning you've lost money the entire decade.

It's the only way to make real money in the long run

Many people have a growing fear of the stock market, but over the long haul, it is still the only way you can make a decent return on your money. If you shy away from the market, there is simply nowhere else to invest. Financial planner Mari Adam says if your only options are CDs, savings bonds or money market accounts, you won't even keep up with inflation. In the United States, the historical annual inflation rate of 3.34 percent means that unless you do something to earn interest on your money, it is going to be worth 3.34 percent less every year. This rate of inflation also means that prices double every two decades, so unless you do something about it, that $10,000 in the bank is going to be worth only $5,000 twenty years from now.

My grandfather liked to tell me he used to pay $.25 for a hamburger back in 1940. Well while that hamburger may cost $6 now, it may cost $18 when you're 70. If you don't do something to try to keep up with inflation, you're going to end up at the register with $6 in your pocket trying to buy an $18 burger.

It's true that you might be able to scrape by just over the rate of inflation with bonds and, during times of high interest rates, CDs, but stocks are the only way to actually make a profit above and beyond that. Consider that from 1926 to 2010, the S&P 500 returned an average annual gain of 9.8 percent. During that same period, long-term US Treasuries returned an average of 5.4 percent.

You can overcome risk and crashes over time

You do have to understand that there is some short-term risk with stocks. There are market crashes—like the 24.4 percent drop in December 1914, the 22.6 percent drop in October 1987 and the

37 percent loss in 2009. But don't be scared away by short-term declines and losses; consider the long-term trends. "A decade like the 2000s was not good for stocks. If you look at just that point in time, the data is going to be very misleading. You have to have a time horizon that is longer than ten years. You have to be thinking about 20, 30 or 40 years," says Adam.

That's scary for some people. You might have watched *Wall Street* and thought you could dump a couple thousand bucks in the market on Monday and turn it into $20,000 by Friday. Well, it doesn't work that way. You have to be in it for the long haul. Your $2,000 investment might be worth $1,800 next year and $1,650 the following year, but in ten years it could be worth $3,500. And in thirty years it could be worth $26,000. Don't let next year's decline scare you away. That's how you have to think.

And yes, it's not easy. According to Adam, when people see a short-term decline or a loss in the stock market, it's all they see. Sometimes that compels people to make decisions based on emotion rather than rationality, which is rarely helpful. Avoid the temptation of a short-term view and force yourself to look at the long-term performance. You'll see why sticking with stocks is the only way you can earn a decent return in the long run.

"It's a problem for some people to see it that way. They extrapolate, they see a decline or loss and that's all they see. They act on emotion and don't use the rational parts of their brain when making these decisions," she says.

Start saving for your kids when they're in diapers

Whether its college, trade school or some kind of continuing education, most parents want to be able to financially help their children with their post-high school plans. Well, the more you can save and the earlier you can do it, the more your kids are going to have. It's just like with your own retirement—you want to use the power of time and compounding to grow your funds, so you can have more while having to put away less.

Save while they're in diapers

Many parents don't begin to save for higher education until their kids are well into elementary school. Unfortunately this means a tough, if not impossible, uphill climb. The reality is that you should try to start saving as soon as they come out of the womb (and preferably before).

As soon as your child gets a Social Security number (which could be as early as 3 weeks after birth) you should open an ESA (Education Savings Account) or a 529 plan. The more you can put away while they're in diapers, the more you're going to have later on and the less you're going to have to worry about when they're in high school. The importance of this can't be stressed enough, because if you keep waiting it's going to be so much more difficult. Even waiting just a few years can make a tremendous difference in how much you put away.

You've got 18 years to let college savings compound

"You're probably looking at an 18-year time span [before] your kids go to college so any money you can put away before they're born or even in those first couple years of life is going to pay off so much more than if you wait until they're eight, ten or twelve," says David Weliver.

Look at it this way: If you were to put away $100 per month starting when your child is one month old, you'd have over $21,600 in contributions at age 18. At a 5 percent growth rate, that would be $38,344 in college savings when they're a senior in high school; 7 percent would be $47,710. Up those contributions to $2,000 per year ($166 per month), earning 7 percent would mean $80,000 to contribute to their college education. That may not completely cover the cost of a college education with living expenses, but it sure as hell beats having only $10,000 put away.

If you wait until your child is 5 and start saving $100 per month, you'll have only $28,000. Compare that to $47,710. Doesn't starting at birth make sense?

Choose the account that is right for you

Aside from an ESA or 529 plan, another alternative is to put those funds in a Roth IRA, assuming that you or your spouse are not currently maxing out your $5,000 limit. So, if you're only planning on putting away $3,000 in your IRA this year, you could open another Roth IRA and put $2,000 in there.

The IRA is a good option if you or your spouse foresee any reason that you might keep the money yourself—if your child decides not to go to college, for example. If that were the case and you had the money in an ESA or 529 plan, you would have to pay taxes and penalties to withdraw the money. Having those funds in a Roth IRA under your name or your spouse's name means it's possible to roll those funds over for your own retirement or to withdraw the contributions tax-free, using the funds as you see fit. The IRA route can be a good option as long as you maintain separate accounts or track which money is for your child's education and which is for you.

It's like anytime else you're trying to save money: Sacrificing a little bit up front will give you more. It's not easy to put a child through college these days, but if you start early enough you'll find it's not all that hard to save. Make it a priority—before the boat or the kitchen renovation—and keep in mind that every dollar you put away when your kids are in diapers could be worth $10 or $20 down the line, not just for education but for the domino effect of the positive financial impact it could have in their life.

Don't put off your own savings

But keep saving. While it's great to be enthusiastic about saving for your kids, Weliver says you should never put their savings before your own retirement. There's a very good reason for that: You can borrow money to send your kids to college, but you can't borrow money to retire. Foregoing your retirement savings, also increases your risk of becoming a financial burden on your kids later in life. And that's the last thing you want to happen.

This further underlines the necessity of saving for retirement as early as possible. Just starting to save for your own retirement *and* your child's education can be an awfully steep hill to climb. "If you can start putting a few thousand dollars away for retirement when you're in your early 20s, it will not only earn more through those extra years of compounding, it will enable you to save more for your kids later down the line," he says.

Prioritize, don't rationalize

When it comes to making purchases and saving your money, it pays to learn to prioritize. Identify what the most important things are in your financial life, and then learn how the decisions you make will impact them.

No financial priorities=possible financial disaster

Nancy Butler says our consumerist culture has made it all too easy to lose track of financial priorities. We're bombarded with ads touting new cars, new clothes, new cell phones and new ways to blow our money, but no one's buying ad space to tell us why we should bank 15 percent of our income. It's not until we understand *why* we need to spend less and save more that we can actually make it a priority.

"People have to really understand and see what their priorities are. They have to realize it, understand it and want it," says Butler. "Unfortunately, many people don't see those priorities—like saving, paying down debt or having an emergency fund—until something bad happens. They get laid off [or they] get into a jam, and then they start making it a priority after the damage has been done."

Don't rationalize bad habits

Even when we know where our priorities should be, we often rationalize our destructive behaviors. We give into temptation once, maybe twice, and then start to think it's not really that big of a deal. What does it matter if you put a $200 purchase on my credit card? You'll pay it off next month, and if not it's only 15 percent interest, right? That's only $30 over the course of the year, or less than three extra bucks you'll pay next month. Or what's the big deal if you forego your retirement savings just this year and put that $5,000 towards a family vacation instead? You've already maxed out your IRA for the past seven years and will continue to do so. You're on track and deserve a break, right?

Wrong. When you take this rationalization too far, you can always find a reason why you don't have to save, why you can spend a little more, why you can incur a little interest. And rationalizing it one time makes it that much easier to do the next time. Not that there's anything wrong with rationalization—as long you're doing it for the right reasons. But when you rationalize destructive behavior or things that can ultimately harm you, you're causing your own problem. And it's too easy to rationalize putting off financial changes until later in life. You tell yourself that you'll start paying down your credit card debt next year, that you'll stop spending less next year, and that by the year after that you'll start putting more money away for retirement.

The truth is that as long as you keep saying you'll do things *later* or *tomorrow*, you're never going to really make a change. There will always be some new commitment, emergency, or expense or other reason why you can't do it. So start now, and start with baby steps if need be. Think hard about your financial priorities and start acting on them.

"Instead of waiting until you're in that situation or facing a problem, why not make those changes now?" says Butler. "Some people have a sense of what their financial priorities should be, but they don't act on them until they're in bankruptcy. And by then, it's a little too late."

Start a side business or find income outside of your day job

You may not realize that you have skills or abilities that can earn you extra income on the evenings and weekends. Michael Friedman says that many people have the ability to turn some kind of skill or hobby into cash. Millions of now-successful small business owners started their companies as little more than a hobby they did after work on the evenings or weekends. Apple was started by a penniless Steve Jobs who built computers in his garage; Dell was founded by Michael Dell in his dorm room at the University of Texas. Like working with your hands? Well, consider that Harley Davidson motorcycles was started as a small garage business in 1901 that built engines for bicycles.

Some skill, talent, hobby or idea you have can make money

You don't necessarily have to take your business that far but you may very well possess skills, a talent or service that can provide a little extra income outside of your day job. And more often than not, what you can offer are things that people have a strong passion for.

"A lot of people have these skills, passions and hobbies, but I think they don't realize the extent to which just a little bit of marketing can actually bring about real cash flow," says Friedman.

If you do want to make money from your hobby, you're going to have to take a few steps into the business world. Start by doing the right research to find out if there's a big enough market to support your business. Discover where your target market is, how big it is and how you're going to reach those buyers. If you have competition, you're also going to have to learn how to do what your competitors do better, which includes playing devil's advocate and truly asking yourself why someone would buy your product or service—or if they even would.

Hopefully what you're interested in can be done as a home-based business on the side rather than quitting your job and taking out a $100,000 loan to buy equipment or lease space. Starting a business is always risky, but if the former option fails your financial loss is manageable, while failure of the latter could take more than a decade to recover from.

The best part about a home-based business or one with minimal overhead is that it's much easier to turn a profit. If you are making a good hourly rate, it should be sustainable. So what if your side business is only making $700 per month? If you're spending 20 hours a month on it, you're bringing in $35 per hour of your time. That's especially good if it's something you *enjoy* doing. The best thing is that you are building income that you *own*. When you work for someone else, you are basically renting that income. And you're in that position until your company decides they don't need you or don't want you anymore, and then you're gone. When you build a business yourself and earn income for yourself, you own that. It's a business.

Draft a business plan

If you're really serious about going into business, you'll have to get serious about business itself. You'll need to have to draft a business plan that will serve as the foundation and roadmap for your venture. It should include everything from start-up costs to lists of necessities to how you're going to market your product or service. You'll also have to do a SWOT analysis to honestly investigate your business plan's strengths, weaknesses, opportunities and threats. Check out this page at the Small Business Administration on starting and managing your own business.

You're also going to have to be realistic and decide how committed you really want to be. What seems like a fun passion now will eventually become hard work, and sometimes even a burden when you have to deal with the business end of turning your hobby into money. But it's the only way you can do it.

Start slowly and don't quit your day job

Whatever you do, test run your business first. Run it on the side, and grow it slowly. Hopefully it's a business that won't immediately require you to quit your day job, because that's an awfully big risk. If you do go that route, you'll want to have a year or two of living expenses saved up, because it's not uncommon for many business owners to go up to a year without paying themselves or taking a salary. This is especially true when you're talking about businesses with substantial overhead like restaurants and retail stores.

According to David Weliver, publisher of MoneyUnder30.com, a side business or some sort of passive income beyond your day job can be a huge financial boost over time. In most cases, people eventually have a cap on how much they can make working for someone else. A rare few will find that the sky's the limit, but at some point, perhaps as early as 10 years into your career, you may find that your income plateaus. Aside from small cost-of-living increases and marginal raises, which may barely keep up with inflation, you're going to find your income stops going up.

"With the exception of highly paid CEOs, there's eventually a cap on how much you can make in your career in the 9-to-5 world," Weliver says. "If you spend a few hours a week turning your passion into something you can sell, "you might be able to turn something into a few extra dollars."

CHAPTER 4

DEBT: THE FINANCIAL BALL AND CHAIN

"When you get in debt, you become a slave." -- *Andrew Jackson*

"Debt, n. An ingenious substitute for the chain and whip of the slavedriver." --Ambrose Bierce

If there's one thing worse than having little money, it's owing money. When a person is in debt and owes more than they have, they have *negative* money.

Every year, it seems, we see well-off celebrities like Mike Tyson, Kim Basinger, MC Hammer, Burt Reynolds, Ed McMahon, Nicolas Cage and Toni Braxton fall victim to their own debts or poor money management. They declare bankruptcy, lose their homes to foreclosure and end up broke.

And if it can happen to these people, it can easily happen to the little guy who makes $40,000 per year. While a $16 million house might drive a celebrity to bankruptcy, regular folks like us could end up in the same situation with just a $175,000 house, a $45,000 car, or $17,000 in credit card debt. When a person lives on a regular income and makes some bad spending decisions that sends them into debt, they can quickly fall into a downward spiral.

For regular people like us, this often starts with credit card debt. And it happens gradually. No one ever wakes up one day, makes a bunch of big purchases and gets themselves into a big pile of credit card debt in a week. It's usually small purchases over a period of time. Maybe you're going out one weekend and decide to throw a nice $120 dinner on a credit card. Three days later you charge $45 worth of groceries, then there's that Netflix subscrip-tion for $15. At the end of the month disaster strikes: Your alterna-tor gives out and you have to tow your vehicle to the mechanic, where you get hit with a $525 bill. That goes on the credit card too. You promise yourself you'll pay the bill in full when it comes, but that $695 seems like a lot of cash to part with all at once. So you make a $100 payment and promise to pay it off in the next three months.

But by then more stuff happens. You charge that, too. And then it snowballs. You got into debt because you didn't have money to buy the things you wanted, and now you don't have money be-cause you're in debt. And it bears repeating: The interest rates on credit cards are killer. They're growing the amount you owe by 17 percent per year. Then you're late on a payment, get whacked with a $35 late fee and you have to pay interest on *that* too. Three months later the bank finds your FICO score has dropped, and combined with that recent late payment, it's enough to up your interest rate to 19.5 percent. Two years later you've got a $2,500 balance on that card.

And you wonder how it happened. The hole just gets deeper and it's harder and harder to get out. Within a couple of years you're so screwed you figure you're so far in debt you may as well just stay in it. And so you rack up more.

Credit cards are the crack cocaine of debt. They're easy-to-get, terribly addictive and destructive tools that are marketed to people who often don't know any better. Credit card companies have long relied on 30-page booklets with tiny print to lay out the conditions and terms of your account. While provisions of the Credit Card Act of 2009 have required credit card companies to be more direct and up front in their terms, you still could fall victim if you're not careful and observant. Financially savvy people are less likely to get into problems with credit card debt because they understand how destructive a 20 percent interest rate can be.

But staying away from credit cards alone doesn't mean you're free and clear. Many Americans have serious debt problems related to their homes and cars. As of late 2011, approximately one in four homeowners were "underwater" in their mortgages, meaning they owed more than their homes were worth. A 2009 study by the Economic Policy Institute also revealed that roughly one in four American households had a zero or negative net worth.

That's a serious problem. Having a negative net worth means your entire financial life is upside down and all of your assets are worth less than what you owe. It means that every day you go to work, every paycheck you collect, every bill you pay, every dollar you have actually belongs to someone else. You're just borrowing that money.

Do you know your net worth and how to measure it? You should. It's roughly the worth of all of your assets minus the worth of all your liabilities—basically, you own minus what you owe—and serves as a quick pulse and measure of your financial situation. You can check out this calculator at CNN Money to see how you stack up with others in terms of your net worth compared to others your age and income.

Then there's student loan debt. According to the Project on Student Debt, two-thirds of college seniors who graduated in 2010 have student loan debt with an average of $25,250. That's not all that bad if you have a good marketable degree that can land you a decently paying job. But the Occupy Wall Street movement has brought to light the fact that there are college grads out there burdened with $50,000, $75,000 and more than $100,000 in debt all for a bachelor's degree in art history—which isn't helping them get a job. People who don't pick their major and university with income in mind and don't have the money to pay for that degree without borrowing can end up saddled with too much debt when they get out of school. If you're already out and thinking about going back for your master's, you should seriously weigh the cost of that degree with the benefit you reasonably think you can get from it. Taking on $75,000 in debt to get your master's in special education when it's only going to up your pay by $3,000 per year may not be a wise investment. You may be doing it because you want to teach, but make sure to also ask yourself if it's worth the financial burden that you're now going to place on yourself or your family.

Aside from refinancing or escalating your payments, there may not be much you can do to deal with that student debt. A magic debt fairy isn't going to swoop in and pay it off.

If you're like most Americans there is a good chance you're already in some type of debt beyond your mortgage and a car note. Factor in student loans and credit card bills and your debt builds and builds until you find that half of your income is going to someone else in the form of interest rates. Your lenders are getting richer, and you are getting poorer.

Once you're in debt, it's less important about how you got there than what you're going to do to get yourself out of it. At times it may seem impossible to pay off all your debts, but plenty of people have done just that. Jennifer McDonough is an administrative assistant and mother of four who helped dig her family out of $120,000 of debt in only 27 months. She chronicles her journey at Fieldofdebt.com and said their problems began when they bought a house "we had no business buying" about 10 years ago.

The McDonoughs were spending more than 50 percent of their income on mortgage payments and, like many Americans, it took them years to realize that they were living paycheck to paycheck, putting little money into savings and living on borrowed time. They had to rely on credit cards and loans from their 401(k)s because they were so far in over their heads, all for unnecessary expenses ($20,000 on a new van, $5,000 on a new boat, $600 to $800 a month eating out), not to mention $15,000 in credit card debt and $20,000 on a home equity line of credit.

When their son was diagnosed with Type I diabetes around 2009, they then had *necessary* medical expenses. And that was the proverbial straw that broke the camel's back. "We were just slapped in the face," says McDonough, attributing their debt to "careless living" and the poorly chosen house. She said they were already squeezed too tight to begin with.

When all was said and done, they had accumulated $120,000 in debt and $25,000 in medical expenses. McDonough said their act of "hitting rock bottom" was a rude awakening, but one that helped them get back on track. "We totally cut any fun out of our lives. We didn't go out to eat, and at the beginning we had a $12 monthly budget for fun and entertainment for a family of five. We [rented movies from] Redbox and did as much free stuff as we could," she said.

The McDonoughs' case may be extreme, but it's an example that everyone can learn from. If they can pay off $120,000 in debt, you can certainly dig yourself out of $15,000 in credit card debt. It takes hard work, discipline, planning and sacrifice, but it is not impossible. Make those temporary cutbacks in life and lower the bar for a little while, knowing that your future will be a lot brighter when you emerge from the tunnel. If you walk around with $15,000 in credit card debt at 20 percent interest, making just the minimum payments it is going to slowly drag you down. Debt is like a cancer; you may not even notice the problem for years before it becomes something you can't ignore.

Understand the difference between good and bad debt

Stuff About Money constantly stresses that overall, debt is a bad thing but yes, there actually are *good* types of debt. Or, if you really want to push it, "less harmful" debt. In a perfect world you would have no debt at all, but there are going to be times when taking on a little debt actually makes financial sense. It all depends on what you're buying, how much of a loan you're taking out and the interest rate you're paying.

Sensible mortgage? Okay.

Financial advisor Kimberly Foss says good debt is usually "a debt that will give you an advantage and greater power down the road."

Good debt is usually fixed, longer-term and used to buy something that will increase in value. Your house is a prime example. Mortgages—assuming you put 20 percent down, snag a decent interest rate and buy a house within your means—are usually good debts. Even in a crappy housing market where values are on the decline, your house is at least going to be worth something if you have to sell it, and in the meantime you can live in it.

"The idea is that by the time you are 60 years old your house is going to be paid for and it's going to be worth more than what you paid for it. It's long-term debt, but it's usually at a low interest rate—and it's an appreciating asset," says Foss.

Sensible car loan? Okay.

Then there are cars. It would be best to pay for vehicles with cash, but most people can't do that. As long as you're buying a reasonable vehicle relative to your income, putting enough money down and paying it off as quickly as possible, that debt is okay too. If a person is making $40,000 per year and borrows $12,000 on a three-year loan to buy a $19,000 vehicle, this might be seen as okay debt. Get a 36-month loan if you can, or get a 60-month loan, then make a couple of extra payments per year.

Loans to start businesses and go to school are also usually good debts because they ideally pay for something that will in turn pay for itself or bring money back to you— assuming you're going for a viable degree or have a solid business plan. Just make sure to measure this debt using a cost-benefit analysis to see if the cumulative cost of what you are borrowing is worth the benefit you'll be receiving.

Then there is the HELOC (home equity line of credit), which can be bad or good debt depending on what you use it for. Using a HELOC to pay down credit card debt, upgrade your bathroom or cover the cost of an emergency? Okay. Using a HELOC to buy a new jet ski and take a trip to Cancun? Bad debt.

Finally we have credit cards, the crappiest of debts on Earth.

There is nothing good about any credit card debt. It doesn't even matter if it's a zero interest rate. It's a credit card, the APR can change at any minute. You can be late on a payment and be hit with a $30 late fee.

Stay away from credit card debt

Credit card debt is one of the worst offenders of wealth degradation. You could dedicate an entire book to how credit card debt can ruin your life. It has run people into bankruptcy, led them to divorce, and prompted health problems and even suicide. These are extreme cases, but at the very least, credit card debt is going to hold you back in life. It's like trying to swim with heavy clothes and a thick pair of boots on; you might be able to stay afloat, but you're going to have to work harder to do it.

Do you really need what you are buying on credit?

Think hard about needs and wants. Using a credit card to help cover the cost of an unexpected auto repair because you didn't have enough in your emergency fund? That's a need. Using a credit card to shop at Nordstrom because you don't have enough money in your checking account to cover it? That's a want. You can be assured that doing the latter on a regular basis is going to leave you with financial problems for the rest of your life.

You may get shafted

Credit cards are designed to screw you. Again—the crack cocaine of the credit world. They're handed out to literally anyone to get them hooked on the lure of easy money and the instant gratification of buying things they can't afford. It's true that some people use their credit cards to pay for emergencies when they don't have the funds, but most credit card debt goes to cover not needs, but wants—the $900 flat screen television, the $120 wardrobe at the mall, the $93 dinner at the fancy restaurant. The fact that you can whip out a card, buy these things now and worry about payment later is all part of the lure. But credit cards eventually screw you with high interest rates, tricky minimum balance payments that extend the time it takes to pay it off, and high late fees.

According to Creditcards.com, American consumers hold 609 million credit cards, with an average of 3.5 cards per consumer. The average credit card debt per household with credit card debt is $15,799, with an average APR of almost 15 percent (as of July 2011). Combined, Americans have a total revolving debt of $793.1 billion—and 98 percent of that is credit card debt.

You had better have discipline

Kimberly Foss says that most people are not disciplined enough to pay their balance in full every month. If you know you fit that bill, it's wise not to even charge anything to your credit card in the first place. She says consumers often fall into the trap of using credit cards as temporary, short-term loans to cover larger purchases between paychecks. The problem with that? If you have to resort to a credit card to fund that purchase, you likely don't have the money for it in the first place. So when the bill comes due, you're tempted to keep a little extra cash on hand and only pay half of the balance. Now you're paying interest and it starts eating into your wealth.

"If you're putting things on a credit card, you're wasting an opportunity to have a better lifestyle down the road. You're robbing from your future and decreasing your quality of life," says Foss.

Moneycrashers.com editor Andrew Schrage says that credit card debt is like a ball and chain that can affect all areas of your finances—your ability to pay other bills, your ability to save, your credit score and, in turn, the interest rates you'll pay and even the insurance premiums you pay. And God forbid you rack up enough debt that you start making just the minimum payments. Doing that with a 20 percent APR will almost guarantee that you'll spend 15 years or more paying off that debt.

The snowball effect

Credit card debt ends up so hard to get out of that people "figure they may as well just stay in it," says Schrage. And so they spend more and amass more debt. It's like the drug addiction that started with a simple hit off of a pipe at a party, just a "one-time thing." Originally, the credit card in your wallet was just in case of emergencies. But then there was the $78 for that birthday dinner; you didn't want to burn the money in your checking account so you figured you'd throw it on the credit card and just pay the balance the next month. But the next week there was the $139 in charges for clothes. Then the week after, your favorite retailer had an unbelievable sale with everything 50 percent off. So you bought $125 worth of merchandise you may not have even needed, justifying it with the fact that you were saving $125. Only you didn't want to draw down your checking account again so you threw it on the card. Finally, at the end of the month your radiator broke, and since you didn't have an emergency fund, you had to put that $380 bill on the card.

The reality doesn't hit until the following month when you get your statement and see that you owe a whopping $722. That number is so big and scary and you don't want to give up the limited funds in your checking account. So you make the minimum payment—and the cycle starts. Three years later your debt has mushroomed; you've found every way possible to rationalize your purchases and you just continue to add to the problem every month.

Foss says it's important to spot that you might be having a problem before you get to that point—not knowing what your balances are or how much interest you're paying and only making the minimum payments could all be early warning signs. "If you can only make the minimum payments on your credit cards, it's already a sign that you have what could become a serious problem," he says.

Not so bad if you use them responsibly

Notice we say stay away from credit card "debt," not necessarily credit cards themselves. While you can now use debit cards to book hotels, order tickets and book flights, there are still times when you might need a credit card or two for emergencies. Having credit cards helps you build your credit, and it also gives you an emergency cushion to fall on when you might not have the funds in your checking account to cover it. The key is to pay that bill as soon as it comes in.

"You have to learn about how to take advantage of all a credit card has to offer without letting it get you in a bad financial situation," says Schrage.

Consolidate high interest bills

Let's say the damage has already been done and you're trying to climb your way out of the credit-card debt hole. In that case, consider consolidating your higher-interest bills. There are a number of options:

Tap a home equity line of credit

Home equity lines of credit (HELOCs) have been one of the best ways to pay down high-cost debt. With interest rates on these loans still near historic lows, that hasn't changed. With a HELOC, you borrow against the equity in your home and get cash. Depending on your credit and income, you may be able to borrow up to 85 percent of the value of the home, including the first mortgage you have in place. So if your home is valued at $200,000 and you have a $155,000 mortgage on it, the max you could borrow with a home equity loan would be about $15,000.

But that's if you're lucky. Due to the recent housing crash, you may simply not have enough equity in your home. The average homeowner now has 38 percent equity in their home, compared to 61 percent a decade ago. And a fourth of homeowners actually have negative equity in their homes.

When you apply for a HELOC, you may have some up-front costs, including a few hundred bucks for an appraisal. So try to figure out if your home's even in the running for a home equity loan before incurring any application costs.

Cash-out refinancing

Cash-out refinancing involves taking out a new mortgage for an amount larger than your current mortgage. Basically, you pay off your old mortgage and use the extra money to pay off your bills.

With mortgage rates also near record lows, this can be a good source of low-cost cash. As with a HELOC, you often have to have 20 percent or more equity in your home in order to qualify for this option; some banks may let you go down to 10 percent.

Let's say you had a bank that was willing to do 90 percent loan-to-value cash-out refinancing. If your home appraised for $200,000 and you had a $150,000 mortgage, you'd be able to borrow $30,000 out of the deal. The bank would write you a new mortgage for $180,000, at which point you'd use $150,000 to pay off the old loan. Then you'd get a check for the remaining amount.

Use a balance transfer credit card or your cheapest existing account

Back in the good old days, credit card companies were so eager for your business they'd constantly offer no-interest balance transfer introductory offers. You could open new accounts, move your debt to a new card every year and pay zero percent interest. If you paid attention to the fine print, you could play the game and win. Nowadays, you've got to look a little harder to find the top deals on balance transfer credit cards. You're also going to have to have great credit. There's the rub—many people who need a good balance transfer card can't qualify for one.

The next-best option is to find an existing account of yours that has the lowest rate on balance transfers. Deals aren't always publicized, so call your other credit card companies and ask if they can offer a better rate to transfer your balance. Sometimes it's as simple as asking.

Go to college but don't take out too much debt

Okay, this isn't a book about college finances. But we can't deny the fact that you're going to make more money and have a better career with a degree. You're likely past your college years but if you're going now or going back for another degree, you should think hard about the debt you could incur.

According to The College Payoff, a 2011 study by Georgetown University revealed that people with a bachelor's degree earn 84 percent more over a lifetime than high school graduates. It also found that on average, a doctoral degree holder will make $3.3 million over a lifetime, compared to $2.3 million for a college graduate and $1.3 million for those with only a high school diploma. It also found that an estimated 63 percent of all American jobs will require some sort of postsecondary education or training by 2018.

How much should you pay for your education?

While there are many reasons for you to go to college, you should also pay attention to how much you pay for college and what you study. Recent studies argue that paying too much for private college tuition or taking on too much debt can make college a hoax. There's some merit to that and you should also weigh the cost of a degree with how much you'll return.

Mari Adam of Adam Financial Associates says a good rule of thumb is to not take on more debt than what you plan to make your first year. So, if you're expecting to make $50,000 per year out of school, don't take on more than $50,000 in student loans. Another rule of thumb is that student loans should not constitute more than 10 percent of your income.

"Before you get your doctorate in philosophy, think about what you're going to do with it," says Adam. "It's a lot more fun to be able to pay your rent and your car note than to be living in mom's basement when you're 40."

You CAN put a price on a college degree

In recent years, countless parents and kids have been taken in by academia's big lie: "You can't put a price on a college education." You most certainly CAN put a price on a college education, and you shouldn't spend, and you absolutely shouldn't borrow, more than the career you're preparing for can justify.

You don't have to look far to find grads with $50,000 in student loans and a job that pays so little they can barely keep up with the monthly payments. Student debt increased from $80 billion in 1999 to $550 billion in 2011, and 11.2 percent of all student loans are now delinquent. Graduating with a mountain of debt into a career that doesn't pay nearly enough to support it can make you a financial cripple for the rest of your life.

And things are getting worse. College tuition has been rising faster than health care costs, and good jobs are getting tougher and tougher to find right out of college. We understand that college is about more than just getting a job and making money. It's about learning, self-development and personal growth. But your college education should make a positive contribution to your net worth, not send you to the poorhouse.

Do a cost-benefit analysis

Doing a cost-benefit analysis can help you decide whether earning a degree is worth it. Consider what you plan to study, how marketable your degree will be, the cost of tuition and what you can expect to make. Start by taking a look at the U.S. Department of Education's College Navigator, which allows you to see the full cost of attending virtually every college and university in the country.

If you're not sure how the tuition at the schools you're considering, the new College Affordability and Transparency Center ranks the cheapest and most costly colleges for you. You shouldn't choose a school based solely on how much it costs, but price should be a major factor in your decision. Look for value in a university.

Now check the National Occupational Employment and Wage Estimates report by the U.S. Department of Labor. This will provide a rough estimate of how much you can expect to make after you graduate and land a job in your chosen profession. Want to be an elementary school teacher? They earn an average of $54,330 a year. Family social workers make much less, with an average annual salary of $43,850, while mechanical engineers earn much more, taking home an average $82,480.

Now you should weigh the costs of your education against how much you're going to borrow and how much you can expect to make out of college. As previously mentioned, you shouldn't take on more debt than you can expect to earn in your first year out of college. But in this day and age, you should probably take on less debt than that. We don't have to tell you that the job market is bad. You can get three degrees and still not have a job. You might want to be prepared for not being able to get a job in your field. And even if you graduate in the top of your class, you may very well make a lot less than you expect to. According to the "Winter 2011 Salary Survey" by the National Association of Colleges and Employers, the average offer to a 2011 bachelor's degree graduate is $50,034. But this survey is skewed; the data comes from university career services that place graduates in jobs—the best jobs. It doesn't account for the tens of thousands of students that got jobs outside of the system or didn't even get jobs.

Be realistic

Let's assume for a minute that you WILL get a job immediately when you graduate. If you do manage to get a decent job straight out of school, you might realistically end up with an average salary of $35,000 to $40,000 per year. Possibly less. Now let's say you took on $120,000 of student debt to attend that prestigious private university. Even if you extend the terms to 30 years, that $40,000 salary means you'd still have to make payments of $720 a month if your interest rate is the current 6 percent. That's a whopping 21 percent of your gross salary that you'd have to put toward your student loans. And even if you get a better job in a few years and make $60,000, you'd still be dedicating 14.4 percent of your income to student loans.

Having to allocate that much of what you make to paying off student debt is going to affect everything else in your life. It is highly unlikely that you'll be able to buy a home or save much for retirement if you're carrying this debt and income. Your life will be set back years, if not decades.

It bears repeating: Your financial life is a marathon, not a sprint. Think about where you're going to be 10, 20, 30 years from now. The cost and benefit of your education determines where you'll start the race.

Is private college too expensive? Probably so. Then go to a public college. Go to a community college. Go to trade school. The point remains that developing something beyond a high school diploma will carry you much further in gaining your financial independence. If your heart is set on a degree from a four-year college, use this tip of Adam's: take your basic classes at a community college, then transfer over to a bigger institution when you're ready to dig into your major.

Use a HELOC to pay down higher-cost debt

You'll hear this over and over in *Stuff About Money*: Credit card debt sucks. It's like trying to swim with a bowling ball chained to your foot—you might be able to keep your head above water but it's always going to hold you down. And at some point it may very well kill you.

You should do whatever you have to get rid of that debt. When you can't pay it off fast enough and the interest rate is very high, tapping a HELOC, as we've mentioned, may be a good option. If you're carrying $5,000 in credit card debt at a rate of 20 percent and can tap a HELOC at 6 percent, that can be a good solution. In a perfect world, you'd never tap a HELOC to pay down credit card debt but if you're disciplined enough, it may be the only reasonable way out.

Before you even think about going this route you need to:

- Make an unwavering commitment that you will not rack up more credit card debt. Otherwise you'll just end up with more credit card debt *and* a HELOC.

- Understand that you are now placing your home at risk. If you default on a credit card they can't come after your home, but they can if you default on a HELOC.

In the example above, if you are making the minimum payment (usually calculated as interest plus 1 percent of balance) every month, you'll be paying $133 per month. It will take 23 years to pay off your balance and you will pay a whopping $7,700 in interest. But let's say that you could make payments of $200 per month. That would cut you down to 33 months of payments, with a total of $1,522.15 in interest.

If funds were tight and you honestly could only come up with that $133 per month, you still might be able to save a lot with a HELOC. If you transferred your balance to a HELOC at a 6 percent rate, you'd be able to pay off that $5,000 in 42 months and it would only cost you $552 in interest. You would not only pay off your debt 19 years sooner, you'd save almost $7,200 in interest.

Kimberley Foss says that it might be okay to use a HELOC for this purpose, but you had better be committed to staying out of debt. Unless you change your habits you'll likely end up in the same situation again. "Make sure you pay it off in 5 to 10 years, have an automatic deduction from your checking account and cut up the credit cards. Put that ugly number on the refrigerator. You're going to see it every day and never want to get into that situation again," says Foss.

Don't apply for too many credit cards

As long as you don't rack up debt on your credit cards and pay the balances in full, there's no harm in opening lots of accounts. Right? Wrong. Opening too many accounts can put a serious dent in your credit score. Each time you apply for a credit card, your credit score temporarily dips about 10 to 15 points.

Credit score formulas penalize borrowers who use more than 50 percent of their available credit. So, if you're opening up a new credit card account strictly to get a discount on some merchandise or to get a few rewards, it could backfire on you. So how many credit cards should you have? Experts say no more than six. A reasonable credit card portfolio might include an Amex, a Visa, a MasterCard, one or two rewards cards and perhaps a gas station credit card (though these are losing their relevance considering you can fill up with a Visa, MasterCard or Amex too). Even that could be considered a lot. Most people may be able to get by on two credit cards—one that they use on a regular basis, and another for backup.

Stay away from store credit cards

Whatever you do, avoid store credit cards. Admittedly, that's not that easy. Just about every store hawks its own credit card these days. Retailers try to lure you into applying with gifts, discounts and offers of no-interest payments for up to a year. But there's no reason to have them. They usually have higher interest rates, their reward programs aren't that great and their fine print can snag you with penalties, retroactive interest charges and all kinds of nasty things. Research shows that shoppers with store credit cards tend to spend three times more than other customers. You can also hurt your credit score just by applying—at 10 to 15 points a pop. Store cards also come with relatively low credit limits that can be quickly used up, and credit score formulas penalize borrowers who use more than 50 percent of their available credit.

Have financial goals

Having tangible, identifiable goals can often help you stay out of debt in the first place. Just what those goals are may depend on your age and lifestyle, but everyone should have some goals in common:

- Money to pay your bills and living expenses.

- An emergency fund in place with at least 6 months of living expenses.

- Setting aside at least 10 percent of your take-home pay for retirement.

- Paying off any non-mortgage debt (car loans, credit card debt and lines of credit) as quickly as possible—and better yet, avoiding them in the first place.

Beyond that, you might be saving for short-term goals like a down payment on a house, a new car, a boat, a vacation or a wedding. While it's good to save any money, it's often easier when you can clearly visualize exactly how much you need. Identify your goals—including long-term goals like retirement at age 62 or paying off your mortgage in 17 years—write them down, track them in a budget and open up separate accounts to fund them.

A target to aim for

William Hammer, Jr., a Certified Financial Planner and Vice President of Vanderbilt Wealth Management, says going through life without identifiable financial goals is like trying to assemble a jigsaw puzzle without the box cover. Most people have vague goals but they don't clarify and attach a cost to them. He says all goals need a name, a deadline and a price tag. "You need to have a quantifiable target. Even if it's a WAG (wild-ass guess), that's still better than nothing. Figure out how much it's going to cost, and [that] gives you something to work towards."

A lack of tangible goals will eventually eat away at your financial life because you won't clearly know what you're working for. "Saving $10,000 is not exciting," says Hammer. "But if you have a goal, a price tag and a deadline, whether that be saving to put your kids through college, for vacation or to buy a condo on the beach, it gives you more of an emotional stake and the drive to go after it. If there is no emotional connection, you're not going to care and will eventually lose interest."

CHAPTER 5

INSURANCE: STUFF YOU NEED FOR WHEN SHIT HAPPENS

"The Act of God designation on all insurance policies; which means, roughly, that you cannot be insured for the accidents that are most likely to happen to you."

—*Alan Coren,* English humorist and writer

Okay, there's no point in denying it: Paying insurance premiums sucks. You fork out hundreds or thousands of dollars per year in case something bad happens. And then when nothing bad happens, you don't get a penny back.

The insurance industry thrives on fear—fear that your house will burn down, that you'll come down with cancer, your teeth will rot away, that you'll get in an accident and paralyze someone else from the waist down. And then there is the fear that you'll die and your family will be left with no way to support themselves.

Insurance companies want you to be scared. Your fear of what could happen is what keeps them in business. They'll throw out stat after stat about all the bad things that could happen to you and why you need to protect yourself. The only way you can protect yourself is to pay them some money every month. And if you drive a vehicle or have a home with a mortgage, you're actually legally required in many states to pay this protection money.

Chances are nothing will happen. Chances are you won't get in an accident, you won't come down with cancer and your house won't burn to the ground. But you'll still have to pay month after month, year after year for the rest of your life.

Let's say you're paying $2,000 a year for health insurance, $1,000 a year for auto insurance, $1,200 a year for home homeowners insurance, as well as $300 for flood insurance and $300 for life insurance. Add all that up and you're forking out $4,800 a year to insurance companies just in case something happens. Over the course of 30 years, that's a whopping $144,000 you'll have spent for nothing more than protection and peace of mind. That's more than some people will contribute to their retirement funds.

As much as the entire concept of our insurance industry smells like a scam, it's also a necessity if you want to ensure your financial well-being. Insurance is a necessary evil. You need it to protect your assets. You can work as hard as you want to save money, invest, buy a house and secure your future, but if you don't have insurance to protect it it's all at risk. If you get into an auto accident and seriously injure someone, if you come down with some rare disease or if your house burns to the ground, your entire financial life could be in jeopardy.

"You buy insurance not based on the hardship but on the costs of the hardship. The problem is that if you don't have insurance for many things, the slightest accident, health issue or damage could wipe you out," said William Hammer, Jr.

In the real world shit *can* happen. If it does, everything you've worked for could be gone in a minute. And the only way you can have protection is by having insurance—and enough of it. Having enough is especially critical for auto insurance because there's a good chance that you will get in a wreck or two during the course of your life. In most states, the bare minimum of auto liability coverage will barely cover the cost of replacing someone's vehicle, let alone if you injure or, God forbid, kill someone.

Then there's homeowners insurance. If you have a mortgage, your lender requires you to carry it, but you want to make sure that your deductible and coverage is right for you. As a subset of that, make sure you carry flood insurance. Less than a fifth of American homeowners have it and almost a quarter of respondents in a survey revealed that they thought homeowners insurance covers floods.

Finally, there's life insurance to protect your family or significant other. Joe Pitzl, Director of Financial Planning for Intelligent Financial Strategies, LLC, says that going without life insurance is not even an option because it's one of the best and only ways you can financially secure your family's future. "When you're a young parent or spouse, the biggest asset you usually have is your human capital and your ability to provide an income. When you're gone, it's gone too. You want to help your loved ones. There is no reason not to have it," he said.

Plus, it's foolish not to have it. Term insurance is cheap; in fact, if you're a non-smoker it's so cheap relative to the benefits it can provide you that it's probably one of the cheapest forms of insurance out there. We're talking 20-year, $250,000 policies for as little as $300 per year

You should also learn what types of insurances to skip. For example, don't even think about buying life insurance for your child. This is a total waste of money and a horrible way to save for their future. There's no need for identity theft insurance or mortgage life insurance either. But the rest of them are necessary evils.

Cover yourself with health insurance

We know. The cost of health insurance is through the roof. It costs you an arm and a leg to insure you against the risk of losing an arm or a leg. When you consider the thousands of dollars you'll pay in premiums when it's likely you'll go years without an accident or barely a doctor's visit, you may even question if it's even worth it. But it is.

Health care is freaking expensive

It takes only one slip down the stairs, one miscalculation when you're driving, one night of unprotected sex or one bad stroke of luck and you could end up with tens of thousands, possibly hundreds of thousands of dollars in medical bills. It's not that farfetched. Medical care costs a lot. A whole lot. It's why your doctor drives a BMW and lives in an 5,000-square foot house. You can find some average costs of medical procedures in the United States at Health Care Fees. Vaginal birth? $6,500. Hernia surgery? $5,000. Heart attack with major complication? $8,900. Hip replacement? $11,700. Lung transplant? $110,000. And if you do get in a wreck ... chest x-ray? $365. Abdominal CT scan? $3,600. Ride in an ambulance? $600. Oh, and on average you'll be billed at least $800 per night for your stay in a hospital room. One auto accident with cracked ribs, whiplash, an ambulance ride and a five-day stay in the hospital and you could easily be looking at a $30,000 bill.

And God forbid you get something like cancer. A serious illness like that—which strikes people of all ages—can be responsible for hundreds of thousands of dollars in medical bills. And you just don't know if it will happen. The best you can do financially is to prepare and cover the possibility of it.

No health insurance is putting all your finances at risk

William Hammer, a certified financial planner and executive vice president of Vanderbilt Wealth Management, says that you shouldn't even consider going without health insurance. It puts you at serious financial risk. You could lose all your assets or find yourself paying off medical debt for the rest of your life.

And medical debt is one of the biggest causes of personal bankruptcy in the United States today. According to a study by the American Journal of Medicine, medical problems contributed to 62.1 percent of all bankruptcies in 2007. Of families that were bankrupted by illness, those with private insurance reported average medical bills of $17,749 while those who were uninsured had an average of $26,971 in medical costs. The highest out-of-pocket health expenses were neurological ($34,167), diabetes-related ($26,971) and injuries ($25,096). You noticed that last one, huh? Even if you think you can't get cancer or have a heart attack, you sure as hell know that car accidents happen to everyone.

"Medical costs are crazy and if you have to pay them out of your own pocket it's going to kill you," says Hammer. "If you are young and are thinking about not having it, just get anything. A crappy policy is better than no policy."

Cheap, crappy health insurance is better than no insurance

If you have health insurance through your employer, consider yourself lucky—and you're welcome to skip the rest of this section. If you qualify for Medicaid that might be nice too, though we're sure you'd rather have more money. If neither of these apply, you're basically screwed. While it doesn't mean you can't get insurance, it does mean you're going to have to pay a lot for it.

As Hammer says, at the very least try to get yourself some type of catastrophic coverage. This is bare-bones, no-frills health insurance that will kick in and cover you if you have a serious health problem. They're usually officially known as HDHP (high-deductible health plans) and feature very high deductibles and are usually paired with a health savings account. These plans are just good enough that if you get into some kind of catastrophic accident, at least the medical bills won't bankrupt you. And they usually won't cover regular doctor visits and routine procedures—just disasters.

"It sucks to have to pay high health insurance premiums and younger folks are the part of the pool that are overpaying relative to other people. But you can't do without it. Your entire financial stability and future can be put at stake," says Hammer.

Protect your income with disability insurance

While life insurance is critical to protect your family, you only die once. In the meantime, you can probably bank on the U.S. Census Bureau's statistic that one in five workers will suffer a short-term disability at some point in their career. Whether it's a car accident, a broken leg from a weekend of skiing or a mysterious illness that puts you in bed for a month, any disability can have a crippling impact on your finances when it puts you out of work. And even if you have those six months of living expenses socked away, the more severe your disability, the more likely it is that you'll run out of money.

Covers you when you can't work

The best way to protect your income is with a disability insurance policy.

Short-term disability insurance (STD) typically covers a percentage of your salary and puts money for living expenses in your pocket should you become temporarily disabled and can't work. It typically covers your income during extended illnesses and hospitalizations, off-the-job accidents and pregnancy and maternity leave

Kevin M. Lynch, Assistant Professor of Insurance at the American College, says that these policies are typically purchased by employers at no cost to the employee. It a number of states, employers are even legally required to provide it to their employees. Coverage kicks in anywhere from zero to 14 days after being disabled and can last up to six months. Lynch says it is important coverage to have to protect your income when personal disaster strikes. "When I am helping someone get their financial plan in order we always talk about emergency funds. Short-term disability can partly cover your living expenses in the event of an accident."

Short-term coverage

Short-term disability insurance isn't meant to replace emergency savings to cover things like job loss or a broken water pipe, but it can really help in the event of an accident that puts you out of work. Most policies pay 60 percent of your salary, up to a cap of $500, $1,000 or even more, depending on your policy. Elimination periods (the time you need to wait to draw benefits) and the benefit period (the length for which benefits are paid) can vary dramatically by policy. Most larger companies with more than 50 employees offer short-term disability for no cost to their employees. Smaller companies may not offer it or will offer it on a group basis, with employees footing the premiums. Premiums are typically determined by the type of industry; the age, gender and characteristics of the employees; and the size of the group.

Short-term disability insurance is especially important for women who plan to get pregnant. The coverage can help cover the loss of income while on maternity leave. The Family and Medical Leave Act requires that employers give their employees up to 12 weeks of leave for the birth of a child—but that leave is unpaid.

If you don't have short-term disability insurance through your employer or are self-employed, finding coverage can be difficult. And when you do find it, premiums can be prohibitively expensive. The individual market for STD coverage is not readily sought after by many insurers and those offering individual policies are few and far between. Mutual of Omaha is one of the few insurers offering short-term policies to individuals. You can save significantly on premiums by going with longer elimination periods and shorter benefit periods.

If you can't get coverage, the best alternative is to self-insure by putting away additional emergency funds—up to twelve months of living expenses.

Long-term coverage

Alex Forrest, vice president of AC Forrest Insurance Group, says you should also consider long-term disability insurance. "Long-term disability is a significant risk that most people are just not thinking about," he says. "We insure our health and wellness and against death, but we don't think about what could happen if we could no longer earn a living."

Long-term disability insurance is designed to kick in once your short-term benefits run out. Policies and periods vary widely, but before deciding on one you should first find out how much short term coverage you have, since it only kicks in when your short-term insurance runs out. There's no reason to get a long-term disability policy with an elimination period of, say, 60 days when your short-term covers you for up to six months.

A combination of long- and short-term

Some insurers are also moving towards hybrid policies that lie somewhere between long-term and short-term disability insurance. These plans are technically long-term disability policies with short-term benefit periods of as little as two years. Long-term policies can be very expensive, Forrest says, so he recommends trying to cover yourself for two to three years. If you're having that serious of a disability, Social Security should kick in by that time.

Protect your loved ones with life insurance

It doesn't matter if you're 28 years old, single, and childless. You should still seriously consider buying life insurance because it is so darn cheap when you're young and healthy. And locking in a 30-year-policy now makes a whole lot more sense than waiting until you're 38 and expecting your first child.

Think about your family

According to research from the University of Virginia's Darden School of Business and Genworth Financial, almost 70 percent of single parents with children living at home don't carry life insurance. Not only that, 45 percent of married parents with children in the household don't carry life insurance either.

If you do have a child or spouse and you *don't* have life insurance, you need it. You know you need it. Without life insurance you're leaving a large financial hole that could jeopardize your family's entire future. If something were to happen to you tomorrow, wouldn't you want to leave behind more than the $8,000 you have in your savings account? You wouldn't be around earning an income anymore, and they'd still have to pay the bills. God forbid you're a single parent, it's even more important.

Term insurance is actually dirt cheap

Gregory Bucko, Director of Customer Innovation at Genworth Financial says there is a common misconception that life insurance is expensive. It's not true. Term life insurance is one of the cheapest insurance products available. For a 30-year-old non-smoking male, a $250,000, 20-year policy should cost $200 per year—yes, per year—or less. Is $20 a month really "too much" to secure the financial future of your loved ones? I didn't think so. Life insurance is about more than just leaving behind a few bucks, it's about solidifying your legacy and taking care of the ones you love. Maybe you have an ailing mother who might need your help someday or a disabled sister who has a hard time making ends meet. Yes, bad things can not happen to you.

"The insurance is there to help your family continue to live," says Pitzl. "When you are young, the biggest asset you have is your human capital, your ability to earn money for yourself and your family. When you're gone, that income disappears."

Figure out how much you need

So how much life insurance do you need? Many factors come into play, but a general rule of thumb says that you should have between six and 10 times your annual income. So if you're making $40,000 per year, you should aim to have between $240,000 and $400,000 in life insurance. Where you pick your number should depend on how much your mortgage is and how much your household monthly expenses are. You should also factor in debts such as car loans and credit cards, as well as the cost of children's college. You may be able to carry less depending on the money and retirement assets you own. And—although this may sound morbid—you'll want to factor in the cost of your own funeral.

The idea is that should something happen, you don't want your family to suffer financially. You want your loved ones to know they have enough money to pay the bills and comfortably take care of themselves. The last thing you want is for them to compound their grief by worrying about how they're going to cover the mortgage.

Pitzl says if you don't want to buy one big policy, you can buy two or three and create a "layered" life insurance plan that will cover you for thirty years. That could include a $100,000 30-year plan, a $100,000 20-year plan and a $100,000 10-year plan. So, in the first ten years you'll be insured for $300,000; between years eleven and twenty, you'll be covered for $200,000, and in the last ten years you'll only be covered for $100,000. The reason the coverage declines is because as you grow older you'll have more assets to leave behind; the hope is that by the time you are 60 you should have a few hundred thousand dollars in the bank.

The draw of layered plans like this is that they can cost less than one big policy. "You project your need based on today and at several breakpoints in the future. It could cut the premiums in half and maybe allow you to afford more coverage earlier on," he says.

You may think life insurance doesn't matter if you don't have much money to begin with. In fact, life insurance is even more important if you don't have or make much money because it will help your family that much more should something happen to you. You may not want to think about these things, but you have to; you owe it to yourself and your family.

Even if you're single and unattached, get yourself a policy while you're young. You could name your parents or siblings as beneficiaries for now, then make a change later if you settle down.

Check out web sites such as www.insurancequotes.com or www.einsurance.com to compare rates and get an insurance quote.

Don't "invest" in whole life insurance

Now that we've addressed the fact that you need life insurance, we need to mention whole life. At some point in your life someone will try to sell you into the idea that a whole life insurance policy is an investment in your future and a great way to save. Walk away.

These policies are very expensive

Whole insurance will cover you for the rest of your life. With that type of policy, a portion of your premium will go towards the insurance cost of your death benefit, the other part will go towards a savings plan in your policy. Salespeople will try to convince you of the benefits of the savings part (also known as "cash value") but don't listen to it. Your premiums will be so much higher and the return on your savings part will be so minimal that you'd be better off buying term insurance and investing the difference.

These policies also come with up-front hidden commissions that could be as much as 100 percent of your first year's premium. You also can't determine exactly what your rate of return will be and how much of what you pay goes towards the insurance and how much goes towards the savings component.

You could do better with your money

The worst part about whole life is that you're diverting money that could be better invested elsewhere (like in your IRA, 401(k) or stocks). You're putting it in a place that not only has a marginal return but high expenses. The salesperson isn't interested in your financial best interest, he just wants to earn a commission. And an increasing number of insurance agents don't even recommend it, which is saying something.

"Your rate of return is going to be a lot better in the stock market than with whole life, particularly when you consider the higher premiums you're going to pay with a whole life policy," says Henderson.

Alex Forrest says whole life insurance typically only makes sense for those who have a sizeable estate and want to shield some assets from taxes. But I'm going to assume that if you're reading this book, you're not one of those people.

So what's the alternative? Henderson recommends that you buy term insurance, which is dirt cheap—about $20/month. The downside with term insurance is that it does eventually end, at which point it may be cost-prohibitive to renew. But if you're 30 now and buy a 30-year policy, you should have enough saved by the time you're 60 that you won't need a life insurance policy. Or at least not a big one.

Save big with term insurance and invest the difference

Another advantage of term insurance is that you'll be able to buy three times to coverage for half of the premiums you would with a whole life policy. The difference can be huge. Whereas a 40-year-old non-smoking male might be able to get a $250,000 20-year policy for as little as $300 per year, that same whole life or universal policy could cost as much as $3,000. For the term policy, that would be $6,000 in premiums over the course of 20 years. If you went with the whole life policy, at the end of 20 year you would have paid about $60,000 in premiums. Of course, you would have a savings portion of the policy that could produce a substantial cash value. The problem is that it's hard to get a true picture and projection of what that cash value could be when you buy the policy. But let's say that 60 percent of your premiums went to the savings portion of the policy and that it grew by 4 percent. In 20 years, the cash value of that policy, which you could surrender or borrow against, would be almost $60,000.

That sounds good until you figure what you could have done had you invested the difference in the annual premiums between the term policy and the whole life policy. Had you invested the $2,400 per year you're saving with the term policy and had it grown at 4 percent, you'd have about $80,000, $20,000 more than you would with the whole life policy. Advocates of whole life say that there are additional tax benefits to such a plan but you could also invest the difference in a Roth IRA and get the same benefit.

"Whole life really only makes sense for someone who has a sizeable estate and wants to shield some of that money from estate taxes," says Forrest. "You're better off just getting a term policy and banking the difference in premiums."

Buy flood insurance

According to a survey by the Insurance Information Institute, only 17 percent of Americans currently have flood insurance. Almost a quarter of those surveyed believed that homeowners insurance covered floods. Financial advisor Mari Adam says she regularly sees clients that aren't aware their homeowners insurance does not cover flood damage. But we all need it. According to the Federal Emergency Management Agency (FEMA), floods, including inland flooding, flash floods and seasonal storms, occur in every region of the United States. Adam indicates that up to 25 percent of claims come from areas that are not considered high-risk, meaning that neighborhoods often flood unexpectedly. "The average claim is $48,000 and flooding can do a lot of damage," she says.

Like life insurance, flood insurance is relatively cheap, Adam says. Even in areas of the South that are highly prone to floods and hurricanes, annual premiums could be as low as $500/year. You can find more about the National Flood Insurance Program at www.floodsmart.gov. Enter your address and it will give you the flood risk of your property on a scale ranging from low to high. It will also display your estimated annual premium cost for contents only (good for renters that only need to insure their belongings), building only or building and contents only.

Create and maintain a home inventory

When disaster strikes, a home inventory can make all the difference in ensuring your insurance company can fairly compensate your losses. It creates a permanent record of what you own and how much it is worth. It can get your claim settled faster, verify your losses for your income tax return and keep track of the things you've accumulated over the years.

According to the National Association of Insurance Commissioners, nearly half of Americans don't have an inventory of their household possessions. You can create a home inventory on your own using a spreadsheet and digital photos or check out this home inventory checklist from the NAIC.

Make sure you have enough auto insurance

When you buy auto insurance, the three main coverages are liability, comprehensive and collision. Liability is legally required to drive in 49 of the 50 states. Most states represent their minimum liability insurance as 25/50/20. The first two numbers refer to bodily injury liability limits and the third refers to the property damage liability limit. This would mean that each person injured in an accident would receive up to $25,000 for a total of $50,000 for the entire accident. And you'd be covered for up to $20,000 in property damage that you caused.

Minimum coverage standards vary by state, but in most cases you should opt for more. Failure to do so means you could put your assets (any money you have in the bank, vehicles and homes) at risk. If you cause $100,000 in bodily injury to someone and you're only insured for $25,000, you could be on the hook for $75,000. And it doesn't matter if you don't make much money. You could still be sued—and lose what little money you have.

"Insurance is about making sure that one unfortunate instance doesn't derail your overall financial plan," says Billy Van Jura, owner of insurance firm Birchyard, LLC. "You have to take out enough coverage to cover yourself." He adds that it doesn't cause much of a wreck to rack up a lot of damage. These days simple fender benders can have auto repair bills in excess of $10,000 and personal injury bills of more than $30,000. If you rear-end someone, they may very well milk their light whiplash into tens of thousands of dollars in medical bills and lost wages.

So up your coverage if possible, preferably to at least $50,000/$100,000. The premiums might cost a little bit more but you won't regret it should you cause an accident someday.

Raise your insurance deductibles

Increasing your insurance deductibles—what you have to pay out of pocket before your insurance benefits kick in—is a good way to save a considerable amount of money on your premiums. You just need to evaluate your cash on hand and make sure you have enough money to handle the deductible if a disaster strikes.

Save for the deductible then raise it

Start with homeowners insurance. Policies typically offer deductibles ranging from $250 to $5,000 and what you choose can have a major impact on your premiums. According to Lending Tree, you can usually save 10-12 percent by increasing your deductible from $250 to $500. Increasing it to $1,000 could save you up to 25 percent, and increasing it to $2,500 could save you as much as 30 percent. And if you could stretch your deductible to $5,000, you could save as much as 37 percent on your premiums. Those savings are massive, but it's important to only increase to the number you're comfortable with.

With homeowners insurance, the company will typically issue you a check for the amount of damage minus your deductible. So, if you have $20,000 of fire or storm damage and a $5,000 deductible, you're only going to get a check for $15,000. You'll have to cover the rest.

Many people can't manage it, but if you're able to put away that $5,000 and have it on hand, then you might want to opt for that deductible. If you go just a few years without a claim, you'll likely even make back that $5,000 in savings on your premiums. If you already have an home equity line of credit open, another, although riskier, alternative might be to count on that for your $5,000 deductible until you can bank enough of the savings to have that amount put aside in cash.

Van Jura says it's usually not advisable to make small claims anyway, as multiple claims could make you less attractive to the insurance company, which in turn could increase your premiums. So any claims you make should be darn important. If you're carrying a $250 deductible, you're unlikely to use it for small sub-$1,000 damages anyway, so there's no point in carrying it. Van Jura says homeowners have often made the mistake of using their insurance as a maintenance policy, calling for minor sheetrock repairs from leaking AC units. That can backfire on you through increased premiums.

Consider what claims you would really make on a car

Let's look at car insurance. If you've got a relatively new car with low miles and you usually don't have that much of an emergency fund, you might want to opt for the $500 deductible. But if you're driving an 8-year-old vehicle with 100,000 miles that is only worth $2,000, it makes no sense to carry a $250 deductible. Since the max benefit you'd receive from the insurance company is only $1,750, you'd likely make up those savings in premiums in a couple of years. In that case, it may not even be worth carrying comprehensive and collision at all, unless that coverage is so cheap it's negligible.

Skip these types of insurance

You need homeowners insurance, auto insurance, health insurance and life insurance. Aside from that, others are debatable—and even more you really don't need at all. Don't bother spending money on premiums for these coverages:

- *Life insurance for your child:* Unless your five-year-old is already a famous actor and bringing in a six-figure income, there's no reason to have a life insurance policy on him or her. These are often sold as a way to save for kids' college educations, but you could find much better places to put the money.

- *Identity theft insurance:* You should be concerned about identity theft, true, but there's no need to pay up to $10/month for identity theft insurance. Grab your free credit report every year to look for suspicious activity and set up free security flags to make it difficult for accounts to be opened in your name.

- *Credit card payment protection insurance:* Credit card companies love to try to get you to buy this. Basically, for a percentage of your outstanding balance, they give you a policy that will cover the minimum payments on your cards in the event of death, illness or job loss. Your disability and life insurance should cover those risks, and an emergency fund should cover you for job loss.

- *Mortgage life insurance:* When you take out a mortgage, the bank will more than likely try to sell you mortgage life insurance. In the event you die, the insurer will pay off your mortgage so your spouse or family isn't burdened with it. If you have life insurance, your mortgage should already be factored into the coverage, making this unnecessary.

CHAPTER 6

RETIREMENT: BECAUSE YOU WILL GET OLD SOMEDAY

"A whole generation of Americans will retire in poverty instead of prosperity, because they simply are not preparing for retirement now."

--Scott Cook, Chairman of the Executive Committee of the Board of Intuit

It's hard to convince some people in their 20s, 30s and even 40s that they need to be saving for retirement. At a time in your life when you're busy going to concerts, chilling out with friends, and hanging out at clubs, no one wants to be thinking about cramping their style so they can put away money for thirty years down the road.

According to the 2011 Retirement Confidence Survey by the Employee Benefit Research Institute, approximately 68 percent of respondents said they have save some sort of money for retirement. That's good, but what they have saved isn't very impressive—29 percent have saved less than $1,000; 17 percent have saved between $1,000 and $9,999; and 10 percent have saved between that and $25,000. That totals 56 percent who had not saved more than $25,000 for retirement. Only 24 percent had saved more than $100,000.

The survey also revealed that Americans aren't very realistic about what they need to save for retirement and how much they'll need in their golden years. Only 42 percent of workers had calculated how much they needed in retirement, and 31 percent thought they needed $250,000 or less to live comfortably. Do the math: If you end up with $250,000 in retirement, that's only

$12,500 per year you could safely withdraw. No matter where you're living or how many coupons your clipping, that little bit of money isn't going to support you when you retire twenty or thirty years from now.

Retirement will be here before you know it, and when the time comes you're going to need money to live. In theory you're not going to be spending as much on some things (like housing; hopefully you will have your house paid off), but you're likely going to have to spend more on others. Like health care—medications could cost you hundreds of dollars per month. You might have to pay someone to perform the tasks you may not be able to any-more, like cut your grass or clean your house. You might even have to pay someone for home nursing care—and insurance may not cover it.

So you should consider putting money away, as soon as possible. It's the same refrain: The more you save now, the more you'll earn through compounding, and the less you'll have to save later on. And again, *the* only place you will ever earn enough money to retire is in the stock market. Don't let the fact that we suffered through a crappy decade in the 2000s scare you away. Over the long haul—and we're talking 30 or 40 years—you can expect to earn about 8 percent per year.

"It's the only way to consistently earn money on your money. You have to invest for the long run and not worry about what happens from day to day or what happened this morning," says David Weliver, publisher of MoneyUnder30.com.

Scared to invest or don't know much about stocks? Weliver rec-ommends you start by opening a IRA and making regular contri-butions to an index fund that simply tracks the S&P 500.

You also need to think hard about Social Security. You'd have to be living under a rock for the past decade not to know that our government-sponsored retirement system has serious issues. No one can say for sure what is going to happen, but there's a damn good chance that, at best, you're going to get a little less money than you expect and have to wait longer to collect it. At worst, you could get a lot less money and wait even longer to collect. Anyone under 40 who goes through life thinking that Social Security is going to cover *all* of their bills when they're in their 70s are as blind as Stevie Wonder.

The point is to be prepared to provide more for yourself in retirement than you think you will. Because while your parents may have retired and got a $2,000 monthly Social Security check every month, there's no guarantee that's going to be there when your time comes. The best way to plan for that is to prepare as if it *won't*. At the very least, tell yourself that you'll collect less than you think you will.

But before you act, make sure you have an emergency fund. Jon Pedley, vice president of product management of Bills.com, says you really shouldn't think about investing or putting away for retirement until you have your emergency fund well in place. It's great to be saving in the first place, but by putting away money in stocks or a retirement fund without the safety net of an emergency fund, you're putting all of that at risk.

You also shouldn't be focusing too heavily on funding your retirement if you're carrying a mountain of credit card debt. "You need to have your credit card debt under control first," says Pedley. "If you're paying 19 percent on a credit card balance and earning 5 percent on your investment, you still have a huge negative return."

Know Your Retirement Goal Number

To retire comfortably, you'll need enough savings to replace at least 60 percent, and preferably 80 percent, of your pre-retirement income. If you make $65,000 per year, want to retire about 30 years from now and replace 70 percent of your income for 25 years, you'll need to save—wait for it—$2 million.

This number probably seems shocking and almost impossible. But now that you see what kind of challenge you're facing, use it to motivate all of your future decisions. The cold, hard reality is that only one out of four of you reading this book will actually reach "your number" in retirement. Just remember: Even if you can't possibly save that much, the more you have, the better off you will be. Retiring with half of your goal is a lot better than retiring with none of it. And it also underlines a constant message stressed throughout this book—do your best to save as much as possible as early as possible.

How much can you really expect from Social Security?

William Hammer says to start by figuring out how much you can expect to get from Social Security. You should get a statement in every year that gives an estimate of what you can expect to collect in retirement. If not, check out this calculator to estimate your benefits. If you were born in 1976 and average $40,000 per year throughout your work life, you could expect to collect $1,043 per month at age 62. That's in today's dollars—in 2038, adjusted for inflation, you would receive about $2,857 per month. But remember, if you're younger than 45, there's a darn good chance that by the time you need them, your Social Security benefits are going to be less than they would be now.

"If you're a Gen Xer, you might want to plan on getting a little bit less or that you're going to have to wait longer to collect," says Hammer.

Consider lifestyle and expenses

You also need to take other factors into consideration, such as whether or not your house will be paid for, whether or not you'll be an empty nester (uh, we hope you are by then), and if you'll be moving to a part of the country with a lower cost of living. With all that in mind, take the number you think you are going to need and then start working backwards. If you expect to need $60,000 per year in retirement, that's $5,000 per month. If you really think you're going to get about $2,000 per month from Social Security, then notch that out and you're left with $3,000 per month—or $36,000 per year that you need to come up with in retirement.

Hammer says while it may not be as accurate, a quick-and-easy rule of thumb to determine how much you'll need is to multiply your salary by 20 to 25. So if you're making $40,000 per year, you'll want to aim to have $800,000 to $1 million put away by the time you retire. At age 30 it may seem impossible to save enough money when you're making $40,000 per year, but remember that you may be making twice that 15 years from now.

Use your goal number to discover how much you need to save every month

Now take that retirement goal number and work backwards. If you want to retire with $800,000 35 years from now, and assume that you're going to earn a return of 8 percent, you're going to have to put away roughly $4,400 per year or $366 per month. (Check out some of the calculators at Bankrate.com to help figure out how to best save for your retirement.)

The good thing is that when it comes to retirement, time can work in your favor. The longer you have to save and let your money grow, the larger your nest egg will become. So starting at 22 is going to make it a lot easier than starting when you're 32. The first $100,000 takes the longest to save, and the biggest returns will come in a rush near the end of your working life. Think about it this way: An 8 percent gain on $50,000 is only $4,000, but an 8 percent gain on $300,000 is $24,000. As your portfolio grows larger, each year's gains will grow larger as well. Retiring with $1 million is not impossible, but it's a lot easier to do when you start early.

Start saving for retirement with as much as possible as soon as possible

The younger you save, the easier it is

We know, it sounds lame. When you're in your twenties you want to have fun. You want to buy cool shit, party till dawn, drive a nice car and shop where you want. You don't want to think about putting away money for when you're a grandpa or grandma. Even if you're doing everything right financially, you still feel like you should be able to blow a wad of cash on the weekends. Go ahead and do so—just understand that someday you're going to have grey hair, walk with a cane and not feel so sexy anymore. The last thing you'll want at that point in your life is to have to have to live in a cardboard box under the freeway, eat canned beans and eke by on the measly $1,800 Social Security check that the dysfunctional federal government sends you every month.

It doesn't have to be that way. Many seniors these days live like they're in their 20s. They run marathons, they party on Bourbon Street, they take vacations. Like it or not, you're going to get old someday, and when the time comes, you might as well try to live the good life.

A little bit can add up over time

The best way to do that is to start saving *now*. It doesn't have to be a lot; a little bit is better than nothing. If you're 25 and have a decent job where you can manage to sock away just $150 per month, it can grow to more than a half million by the time you're 65, assuming you earn a return of 8 percent. Bump that up to $200 and you'll have $675,000.

"The earlier you save, the better. Even if it's your first job and you can only start out with $100 per month, then do it. It's about baby steps, taking on step at a time," says Kimberly Foss. "If people can start saving when they're in their 20s, it's going to be so much easier when they get older."

Now, if you wait until you're 40, you'll have to save $550 per month to have a half million by 65. And if you think it's hard to save now, it could be even harder to save later when you have a mortgage to pay and a couple of kids running around. At that point, putting away $550 a month might not be too easy and you may regret not forking out that measly $150 a month when you were in your 20s.

Think about it. $150 per month to have yourself a half million when you're 65. That's not much to ask. Find the money and do it.

And if you're already in your thirties or forties and have little saved for retirement, then it's time to start doubling down. The best part for you personally is that once you start saving for retirement, even if it's only $100 per month, you'll start having a long-term goal and a vision of where you're going. That will lead to you wanting to save more, minimize your debt and make better financial decisions.

No matter how much you can save, the important thing is to just do it, every month. "Start saving in increments that are sustainable. It's about discipline. Saving for retirement teaches you to be financially accountable for yourself in many other ways, says Foss.

Make regular investments and have a long-term view

We've already highlighted why you should be investing. Whether it's in an IRA for your retirement or an individual account simply to try to grow your money, putting at least a portion of your money in the stock market is the only way to grow it. It's okay to start small; you can buy a couple of shares in a solid company for as little as $100. But if you actually want to build and grow a portfolio, you're going to have to make regular contributions.

A small start can add up big over time

If you open an account now with $100 and put away $100 per month, you'll have over $24,000 in contributions in 20 years. But the real joy of stocks comes with the opportunity to grow your money through capital gains and dividends. Often, you'll earn both.

If your holdings grow at an annual rate of 6 percent, in 20 years you'll have over $47,000. And if they grow at 8 percent, you'll have almost $60,000. Get the picture? Little contributions can add up if you make them regularly.

Look for solid companies

Chasing hot stocks and short-term killings based on tips from CNBC or online forums is essentially gambling. Most small investors who leap into a company because of rumors it's a takeover target, or news that it's about to receive federal approval for a new drug, or an announcement of better-than-expected quarterly earnings, lose money on those deals.

You want to build your portfolio around companies that offer steady growth and reliable dividends. That also requires you to resist the temptation to buy and sell on impulse, gut feelings or daily news. Don't dump a stock because it lost 10 percent in a day or had disappointing quarterly results. You're not investing for next week, next month or even next year. Think about where you want your portfolio to be five, seven, 15 or even 20 years from now.

Follow the old-fashioned principles

You should also use some old-fashioned investing principles like buy-and-hold. This entails buying solid stocks in solid companies, then holding them indefinitely or until you need to liquidate your portfolio. Most people buy and hold blue-chip stocks, solid companies that have been around for decades. These stocks tend to be more stable and have less dramatic swings.

Then there is dollar cost averaging. This works well with regular contributions and calls for investing a set amount in the market every month, whether or not the market is up or down. When it's down your money will get you more shares, when it's up, you'll buy less. This prevents you from trying to time the market and minimizes the risk that you'll buy at the wrong time.

Look for dividends

Finally, go for dividends. This means buying stock from solid companies that have a long history of paying and increasing their dividends. A number of solid stocks out there that pay 2.5 percent to 5 percent dividends double what you could earn in a top-paying CD these days. Dividends are typically paid quarterly and can be reinvested to buy more shares. This can dramatically increase your earnings over time.

Start by taking a look at the 30 blue chip stocks in the Dow Jones Industrial Average. These companies are generally leaders in their industry have been around for decades and have strong balance sheets. That means they have lots of cash, little or average debt and very long track records of profitable operations. You can research stocks at your broker's web site. There you can look at analyst ratings, find the latest news on the company and view quarterly reports.

Investors often use the P/E ratio (price to earnings) to value a company's share price. A typical average is 15, meaning you'll pay $15 for every dollar of earnings. A higher P/E could mean the share price is overvalued, a lower P/E could mean it is undervalued.

One could go on forever about the best ways to pick a stock, but buying a few diversified blue chips with old-fashioned principles is likely the best way to start your portfolio. As time goes by, you can then learn more about the market.

Open a Roth IRA

Even if you have a nice 401(k) plan at work, consider opening a Roth IRA. It is one of the only ways regular Joes like us can make tax-free money. And the tax savings can be huge. Unlike traditional IRAs, which are not tax deductible, contributions to a Roth can be withdrawn tax-free at any time.

Tax-free retirement

You can contribute up to $5,000 per year in a Roth. If you were to max that out every year for 30 years and earn 7 percent on your contributions, you'd have more than $540,000. And did we mention that money can be withdrawn *tax-free*?

Some people point out that the disadvantage of the Roth IRA is that contributions are not tax deductible. But Robert Henderson says that this isn't much of a concern for most middle-class investors because the tax savings are marginal. If you're in the 15 percent tax bracket, you'll only save about $750 if you max out your traditional IRA for the year. That might sound like a lot in savings up front, but it's unlikely to pay itself back considering that when that $5,000 has grown to $50,000 in thirty years you're going to have to pay taxes on $45,000 in capital gains. When you go with the Roth, you'll lose that $750 deduction this year, but you'll be able to take your money tax-free in retirement.

"It's a huge advantage because you don't even know where taxes are going to be 30 years from now. The tax deduction is not as valuable as it seems for people in the 15 and 25 percent tax brackets," he says.

It's flexible

Financial advisor Mari Adam says the fact that contributions can always be withdrawn makes it a great option especially for younger people. There's no fear that you can't touch the money for 30 years. You should only tap into it when necessary, of course—like for an emergency. You can also pull up to $10,000 out of your Roth in earnings tax-free if you're a first-time homebuyer and use the money to buy a house.

"Opening a Roth IRA is one of the best financial moves you can make. You can't contribute that much, but it adds up over time and you'll never pay taxes on it," says Adam. "And it gives you that flexibility to where if you do need it in an emergency or for something important, you can access the principal for any reason tax-free and penalty-free."

Build a diversified portfolio

Whether you've got a $2,000 or $2 million portfolio, you do not want to have all your eggs in one basket. It doesn't matter how hot you think a company, industry, region, or commodity is, if you invest all your money in it, you risk losing all of your investment. The best way to manage some of the risk in a portfolio is to spread the risk among a number of companies and sectors.

Spread your risk

Jeremy Vohwinkle of Generation X Finance says putting all your money in one company or industry is like going to a roulette table and putting all of your money on one number. It could pay off, but the odds are largely stacked against you. No matter how many shows you watch on CNBC, how much you read the *Wall Street Journal,* or how great you think you are at picking stocks, you ultimately don't know much. Think about it: If you did, you'd be riding around in your Ferrari now, not reading this book. That's okay. Just know your limitations, and use diversification to spread your risk.

"You really don't know how the market works. With more things in your portfolio and different types of industries, you're going to have a better chance of not losing everything," Vohwinkle says. He recommends diversifying with a mix of stocks and bonds. Bonds typically provide the safety, whereas stocks typically deliver the growth. A common rule says the percentage of your portfolio that should be in stocks should be equal to 110 or 120 minus your age. So, if you're 35 years old, you should have about 75 to 85 percent of your portfolio in stocks.

When it comes to stocks, you don't want to have all of your money in one industry or company. You might think that oil, tech, real estate or gold is riding a wave, but you just don't know when it's going to crash. And if you haven't learned it by now, every bubble eventually bursts. When it does, you don't want to have all of your money in it. So resist the temptation to throw everything into the winner of the day.

A well-diversified portfolio should spread your money—and thus your risk—among multiple companies *and* multiple industries. It might include an oil or other energy company, a tech company, a financial services company and a consumer goods company. If you're starting out small, you won't be able to build a diversified portfolio immediately. Alternate your purchases to buy into the positions you want. You can also opt for instant diversification through an ETF (exchange traded fund) or mutual fund.

Don't day trade

Some people take an interest in CNBC.com, start reading the *Wall Street Journal* and suddenly think they're going to be the next Warren Buffet. It may sound funny, but many people fall under this spell and resort to day trading, believing that something some analyst said is going to make them rich. They drop $5,000 on a hot stock tip, expecting to book a 15 percent capital gain the next day, then dump the stock for a handsome profit.

Admit you don't know anything

The reality is that more often than not, you're going to lose money. And you'll lose a lot. If big-time professional stock analysts with Ivy League degrees can't predict the market, what makes you think that you can? Admit it: You don't know crap. And that's okay, none of us do. Even professional traders that make money with stocks don't claim to know what is going to happen when the market opens. They only know how to better calculate and diversify their risks to minimize their chances of suffering substantial losses. And in the world of day trading, the ultimate goal isn't necessarily to make money, it's to not lose it. Or at least too much of it. Day trading is more than a hunch or a stock tip; it's a complicated plethora of factors that are beyond your control or comprehension—and mine.

There's too much risk

Robert Henderson says that day trading or acting on impulse when investing is a sure recipe for disaster. You never know what tomorrow's news is going to bring. Natural disasters, terror attacks on the other side of the globe, a bad report from an agency, a surprise announcement by the Fed—all of these can all send the market into chaos. Then there's momentum: You jump into a stock because it's up 15 percent in the past week, and you think the trend is going to continue. But two weeks after you buy in, the company's quarterly results miss analyst forecasts, and the stock nosedives by 8 percent.

"They jump on the bandwagon, and what happens next is that the market sinks. To try to predict the direction of the market or a stock based on today's news or yesterday's news is a futile effort," says Henderson.

The best advice is to resist the urge to day trade, and build your portfolio with old-fashioned, time-tested principles. This includes building a diversified portfolio with dollar-cost averaging, regular contributions and buy-and-hold strategies. Build a portfolio that you can hang on to for years and that will grow your money slowly. You *could* make 30 percent on your quick trade tomorrow—but you could also lose 100 percent. It's better to let time, dollar-cost averaging and regular contributions work on your behalf and earn an average 7 percent over 30 years.

If we can't stop you...

You're going to take a risk and day trade anyway? Fine. If we can't stop you, then just keep it small. Very small. If you've got $100,000 in the bank and want to start a day trading kitty with a few thousand bucks, then go ahead. But if you've got $5,000 in the bank and you think you're going to day trade with $2,500, realize that you stand to lose half of your money. You should only day trade with funds that you can afford to lose. Henderson recommends using your "fun money" on such trades, and keeping it to a minimum.

"It's essentially gambling, and the odds are stacked against you. It's very rare that an ordinary person can predict a super investment," says Henderson. "Only do it with money you can stand to lose. Keep your real money in the market with a long-term view."

Take advantage of your employer's 401(k) match

If you have access to a 401(k) at work and your employer has a matching program, you should always take full advantage of the match every year. It's *free* money, likely some of the only free money you'll ever get in your life; you'd be a fool not to take it. Jeremy Vohwinkle says contributing to a 401(k) is the easiest way to start investing. In fact, most employers now automatically enroll their employees in their 401(k) plans unless they fill out a form to decline.

An automatic return

Many employers offer a 50 percent match up to the first 6 percent. That means your employer will contribute $.50 for every dollar you put in, up to a grand total of 6 percent of your salary. So, if you're making $40,000 per year and invested $3,000 in your 401(k), your employer will kick in another $1,200. At the end of the year, despite what happens in the market, you'll have already earned an extra $1,200. That's a 40 percent return on your entire contribution and a 100 percent return on something you can not find anywhere. "At the minimum, you should be working to contribute enough to maximize the match. Even if you have the worst 401(k) in the world with high fees, getting that free money is going to offset that," says Vohwinkle.

Don't be scared off by recent downturns in the stock market. It's true that in 2008 many 401(k) plan participants saw their balances shrink by more than 25 percent, but by 2011, nine out of the 10 popular retirement plans were back to where they were in October 2007 during the peak of the stock market. The investors who continued to contribute are even further ahead. If you have a 401(k) with a match, take advantage of it—it's some of the only free money you'll ever get in your life.

Don't cash out that 401(k) when you leave your job—it will cost you

A 2009 study of 170,000 401(k) participants by Hewitt Associates found that 46 percent of them cashed out their accounts when they left their jobs. This is a massive problem. When you do this you'll have to pay not only personal income tax but a 10 percent penalty for early withdrawal.

When you consider that many workers change jobs five to seven times before they settle into a long term job, cashing out your 401(k) every time you leave a job can cost you a fortune. The fine alone for cashing out $5,000 would be $500, and then you might have to pay another $1,000 or so in taxes. Don't do it. Ask your new employer for the paperwork to transfer your old 401(k) funds into your new account. Or, leave it in you old employer's 401(k) plan; no one can touch that money. It's yours. A third option is to roll it over into an IRA, which is easy to do through any brokerage.

Keep an eye on investment fees and expenses

If you're investing in a 401(k) or IRA (uh, you better be!) you also need to keep an eye on your investment expenses. That's because even 1 percent more in expenses over the course of your career on your retirement assets can have a huge impact.

Over time, even one extra percent can destroy over 20 percent of your portfolio

It's good that you're investing your money and saving, but if that expected 8 percent return over time drops to 6.5 percent after fees and expenses, you'll end up with a lot less money. You can't fully avoid all fees and expenses, but you can certainly be conscious of what you're paying for—and how much you're paying.

Consider that $100,000, over a 30-year period with a rate of return at 7 percent, would grow to $761,000. If a mere 1 percent in expenses were deducted from that account on an annual basis, it would be worth only $574,000 in year 30. That difference equates to $187,000 in fees, minimizing the total return by 24.5 percent. Believe it or not, for a person who actually invests their money and saves for retirement, money management can be his or her third largest expense after housing and vehicle costs. And the impact of those fees, because they are collected in such small amounts, cent by cent, dollar by dollar every day, makes them hard to see. If a fund is performing well, it's even easier for investors to focus on return and not notice the amount in fees that are going out the back door.

Adam Koos, financial advisor and president of Libertas Wealth Management, says it is critical to keep an eye on your fees and recommends that investors stay away from target date funds, not just because they often have poor performance but because also often have high fees. "The average cost of a mutual fund is now 1.6 percent. It is amazing how much of a difference 1 percent can make over the course of decades, let alone 1.6 percent. It can make a huge difference in your portfolio and can be the difference between retiring at 62 and retiring at 70," says Koos.

Look carefully at your statements and double check how much you're paying on any funds you own in your IRA. That said, don't let high fees steer you away from putting money in your 401(k) if your employer has a match. In many cases, that match alone will more than make up for the fees and expenses you'll pay, so contribute at least enough to take advantage of that full match. After that, you can take the remaining funds you'd like to contribute towards your retirement and put them in your own IRA, where you can make your own investment decisions and, hopefully, avoid high fees.

Check your quarterly statements

The good news is that starting in 2012, the Department of Labor required that all employer-sponsored 401(k) plans will disclose all fees on investments and transactions. Investors can usually find expense ratios on the funds they hold, but it's much more difficult to find plan administrative costs like legal, accounting and record-keeping fees. You can usually request this information from your plan administrator, but they will now be required to provide it. You're also now supposed to receive quarterly statements that show the dollar amount of the plan-related fees along with descriptions of what they cover. They must also provide clear performance data, benchmark information, and fee and expense information. The rule will affect an estimated 72 million participants with more than $3 trillion in assets.

Don't count on Social Security

Your grandparents collected Social Security, and your parents will. But there's a very strong chance that at the very least, you'll collect less from Social Security and you'll have to wait until you're older to collect it.

Being financially independent is ideal, because it means it won't matter if Social Security is there or not—or at least it won't matter much. And if it is there, you can think of it as icing on the cake. Currently, over 54 million Americans collect Social Security with an average benefit of $1,076 per month. That isn't that much anyway.

If you think it's uncertain now, what about 30 years from now?

By most accounts, Social Security is projected to run out of money by 2037. So if you're over age 35, that means it will run out before you hit retirement age. What happens then? That could be anyone's guess.

In 2011, Social Security paid out more than $45 billion more[??] than it collected in payroll taxes, according to the Congressional Budget Office. Congress will keep borrowing to fill the gap, but with the federal deficit increasing to $1.5 trillion—and growing—we all have to wonder if something is going to give at some point.

There are bound to be a number of changes to the program in the coming years. First, there is likely to be a smaller cost-of-living adjustment. Social Security benefits are boosted each year to keep up with the Consumer Price Index, but some legislators have suggested switching to another inflation gauge, the "chained" CPI. It is supposed to reflect what real-life consumers do when a product or service gets more expensive.

Replacing the CPI with the chained CPI would reduce Social Security's cost-of-living adjustment by about 0.3 percentage points a year. That may not sound like much, but over the course of 20 years, it means monthly benefits could be about 6.5 percent lower. Instead of receiving $1,800 a month, you might be paid only $1,683. Over the course of an entire year, that would reduce benefits by $1,400.

Another likely possibility is that you'll have to wait longer to collect. Most proposals on the board call for raising the retirement age, as it is a tried-and-true way to cut costs. When Social Security was created, all recipients qualified for full benefits when they reached 65 years old. When Reagan and Congress dealt with the last shortfall in the early 1980s, the retirement age for everyone born after 1937 was gradually raised. It's now a maximum of 67 years for all recipients born after 1959, and budget cutters are proposing to increase the full retirement age to 69 or 70 by 2027 to 2032. Early retirement age—the age at which you can receive reduced benefits—would be raised from 62 to 64 or 65 under most plans.

There's also the possibility that high-income earners may have to pay more into the system. Right now, everyone pays Social Security taxes on their income, but only up to the first $106,800. As recently as the 1980s, that income cap allowed the government to tax up to 90 percent of all wages. But faster-than-expected growth in high-wage jobs has left the government taxing only 86 percent of all wages today, and the pool of taxable income is expected to be less than 83 percent by 2020.

Raising the limit higher would subject more high salaries to Social Security taxes. A number of proposals suggest increasing the limit to $190,000 by 2020, and continuing to raise the cap so that 90 percent of all wages are taxable by 2050.

The last possibility is the most radical solution and the one that is least likely to happen: that they will privatize the solution. This suggestion is based on the long-standing dislike conservatives have for Social Security as a government-mandated redistribution of wealth. They don't think it's right to force workers in their 20s or 30s to support millions of retirees who often collect far more in benefits than they paid into the system when they were employed.

The proposals you'll hear to privatize the system usually seek to turn it into a new system of mandatory tax accounts so that the money you put in there would be used to pay for your benefits, and only your benefits, when you retire.

There is one such program already in existence in Galveston County, Texas. There, employees contribute 13.9 percent of their gross pay (6.1 percent from the employee, 7.8 percent from the county) to a private account that you can invest in as you would with your 401(k) plan. At retirement, they can take the money in a lump sum, arrange monthly payments or purchase a lifetime annuity.

It could be there, just don't put to much faith in it

Social Security has run a surplus the past couple of decades, thanks to the baby boomers, and the extra has been stashed in Treasury bonds to cover some of the extraordinary costs of their own retirement. But fundamentally, it's a pay-as-you-go system that expects younger generations to pay taxes to provide benefits for the elderly.

Jeremy Vohwinkle says most people who try to live on what they can collect from Social Security alone barely live over the poverty line. "Until people see it firsthand, they usually don't understand how little [Social Security] is. Even if you get your full benefits, it's not a way you want to live. Thing of it as a bonus, not bread and butter," he says.

The bottom line is this: Do you want to put that much faith in Social Security? Do you really think that in 35 years there's going to be money for you?

The experts say don't count on it. Save, put away money and plan as if it *won't* be there. If it isn't, you'll thank yourself. If it is, you might end up receiving an extra $1,800 per month. Either way you'll come out a winner.

CHAPTER 7

VEHICLES: DON'T DRIVE YOURSELF TO THE POORHOUSE

"I had more clothes than I had closets, more cars than garage space, but no money."

—*Sammy Davis, Jr.*

We've got to dedicate an entire chapter to vehicles because for many Americans, their car is their second biggest expense in the budget, just behind their house, and can suck up a large portion of their income. Most financial advisors say a good rule of thumb is to not spend more than 10 percent of your take-home pay on a vehicle.

In general, to optimize your long term financial security, growth and stability, we should buy the most inexpensive reliable vehicle we can, then drive it for as long as we can. But when most people get to the car lot, a lot of that goes out the window.

Joe Pitzl says that there is a strong mental element in buying a vehicle that is more about emotion than utility. Very few people ultimately make their car-buying decisions based on practicality and finances. In many cases it comes down to how the vehicle makes them feel—happy, successful, prosperous—or the outward appearance they think the car projects. "People have a tendency to fall in love with vehicles, but [after] you buy that new car and drive it around for a couple of years you're going to see something cooler and want a new one," says Pitzl.

The problem comes when that new car is more than you can afford. At some point, all new cars are no longer new. If we give in to the "new car every three years" mindset, it becomes a neverending cycle of depreciation, taxes, and other expenses that just suck your money down the drain.

There's nothing wrong with having a love for cars, just be sure you have the income to support it. By buying too much car too often, you could be robbing yourself of other important financial obligations like saving for retirement or paying down debt. We all know those people who drive $50,000 vehicles, then claim they have no money to save for retirement, or complain that they can't afford health insurance or that their credit card bills are too much to deal with. Juggling too big of a car note will always impede your ability to handle other financial obligations in life.

At worst, a new car can send you straight to the poorhouse. If a person is making $40,000 per year and buying a $40,000 Chevy Suburban, they will eventually, somehow, somewhere down the line, pay a hefty price for owning that vehicle. Let's say they put down 10 percent and finance $30,000 at 8 percent for 5 years. That gives them a monthly note of $600. They might think you can juggle that, and they may very well do it, but it's at the expense of other important parts of their life, whether they realize it or not.

If that was you, say you decide you could drive a smaller or less expensive vehicle and knock your car note down to $200 per month. That's $400 per month extra you could have for building your financial cushion. Over time that can seriously add up: a savings of $4,800 per year, or $24,000 over the life of the five-year loan. "Locking yourself into a big car payment robs you from saving money. And not only that, you're preventing yourself from spending money on things like vacations that you are going to remember a lot more than you car," says Pitzl.

Whatever you do, be sure to drive your vehicle as long as you can, at least until reliability becomes an issue. Danny Kofke, who supports himself, his wife and his two children on a salary of only $40,000, is living proof that having a paid-off vehicle can free up a lot of space in your budget to save or do better things with your money. Not only does he cover the bills, he still manages to save money for retirement and his children's education.

"Not having a car note is amazing," he says. "Cars get a lot of people in trouble. If you really want to get ahold of your finances, drive [your car] as long as you can until the repairs are not cost-effective."

Don't overspend on a vehicle

A common rule of thumb to use when buying a vehicle is the 20/4/10 rule. It says that you should put at least 20 percent down, finance the vehicle for no more than four years, and not spend more than 10 percent of your income on the monthly note.

Be honest about what you can afford

We're not recommending that you buy a junker. But if you're making $35,000 per year, it may not be the best financial move to buy a $30,000 vehicle. You generally shouldn't be spending more than 10 percent of your gross annual income on a car or truck, including payments, insurance and maintenance. That's only about $300 per month.

If insurance is going to run you $125 per month (and it may very well in some states if you're under 25), that gives you $175 per month to spend on a vehicle. If you can snag a five-year loan at 6 percent, that means you can borrow up to $9,000 and stay in your budget. That gives you a total of $14,000 to work with. You should also factor in the "true cost to own" of the vehicle, which you can do at Edmunds.com.

Will $14,000 get you a brand-new car? No, but it should get you a pretty decent pre-owned one. If you want to have financial strength and stability in your life and you're not making enough bucks, you're going to have to make smart decisions. Buying more car than you can afford compromises other parts of your financial life—your savings account, your emergency fund, your retirement account, paying down other debt and preparing for your future. While it may be fun to have that new shiny car, you're going to pay for it in a number of ways down the line.

It will improve other parts of your financial life

It may not seem like a big deal to overstretch on that $30,000 vehicle when you're 25. But six years later when you have a baby on the way and little in your savings account, you'll wish you hadn't put so much money into a vehicle that has since been sucked away in depreciation.

Jeremy Vohwinkle recommends spending as little as possible on a car. "A car is literally a hunk of metal you use to get to work," he says "People have to get past the idea that they need a $60,000 SUV to drive back and forth to work. It's really just an image thing."

Overspending on a vehicle isn't just about the sticker price. It's also that you're likely to borrow more, and at a higher interest rate, further increasing the total price of the vehicle. And don't forget that a more expensive vehicle will demand higher insurance premiums. If you buy a $30,000 vehicle, put down only $5,000 and take a five-year loan at 6 percent, you'll end up paying over $4,000 in interest by the time it's paid off. That means you really spent $34,000—for short-term gratification on a bill that will come due later in life.

Consider the whole cost of the vehicle

Still, many people stretch their budgets as far as they can to buy the car of their dreams. They might be able to squeak by and make the monthly payment, but fail to factor in the whole cost of the vehicle, which go well beyond the sticker price. A Consumer Reports study of more than 300 vehicles found the major costs of vehicle ownership to include: depreciation (46 percent), fuel (26 percent), interest (12 percent) and insurance (10 percent). Most people don't give much though to depreciation, but vehicles depreciate rapidly; the average model will lose over 65 percent of its value in five 5 years. That means five years from now, the

$27,000 vehicle you're looking at will only be worth about $9,400.

This should underline why it's probably not the best financial decision to buy new cars, then only hold onto them for four years. By then you've already taken a major hit on the value of the vehicle, so if you turn it around, you're going out and taking another big hit of depreciation on another vehicle. Since you've already lost a third of the vehicle's value in depreciation, shouldn't you go ahead and drive it a few more years?

Finance as little as possible on your vehicle

Never, ever, under *any* circumstances, take personal finance advice from a car salesman. They have no interest in your long-term financial future; their only concern is getting a commission on the sale. They couldn't care less if your vehicle purchase later puts you into financial trouble in other parts of your life, or even if your car gets repossessed six months down the road. Their job is to make money to support themselves and their families—just like yours.

Lower monthly payments don't always equal a better deal

Understand that there are two main parts to an auto sale: the price and the interest rate. A car salesman is always going to get you to focus on the price and the monthly payment. Because most people don't do the math, they think they're getting a better deal when they get a lower monthly payment.

Not true. Look at the interest rate, price and the total payments. Fortunately with today's truth-in-lending disclosures, you'll usually be able to see a total cost of the vehicle on the paperwork. But you'll have to look very closely.

Dealers will always try to make the deal about the monthly payment, because it's the easiest way to play you for a fool—they know that most people don't even understand how the numbers mesh together. Don't tell them what kind of monthly payment you can afford because they'll use that number to sell you a more expensive car or truck than you may have wanted, maximizing the dealership's profits. The salesperson will figure out the most you can possibly spend by dragging out the payments for as long as possible and still hit that payment. He or she will then show you cars and trucks in that price range, which is often higher than what you wanted to spend, while reassuring you that this fine vehicle is within your budget.

Let's say you come in to buy a compact sedan that costs about $20,000 but let slip that you could afford a payment of $450 a month. The salesperson immediately recognizes that a 60-month or 72-month loan would allow you to buy a $25,000 midsize sedan and your payment would still be about $450 a month—and that is what he or she will try to sell you.

There are only two ways to finance less: put more money down or have a lower price.

Look out for the tricks

During negotiations, your salesperson may say he or she can offer you a lower price if you'll finance the purchase through the dealership. That's a sign to be very careful. Your salesperson may be hoping to recoup any discount in price through a finance charge mark-up. That's when the dealership adds 3 percentage points—sometimes more—to the interest rate one of its lenders is willing to charge you.

Applying for a loan through the car dealership means sending your information to the finance companies that it regularly works with. These lenders check your credit history and come back with their best offers. One may say you're eligible for a loan with a 7 percent annual interest rate. Only the car dealer tells you the rate is 10 percent.

On a $22,000, five-year loan, that extra 3 percent adds $1,908 to your payments. The lender collects that money and sends anywhere from half to all of it back to the dealer.

Drive your vehicle as long as you can

Automotive marketing research firm R.L. Polk found that Americans are keeping their cars an average of 52.2 months. There's no reason to replace today's vehicles after just four years. Many people wisely decide to drive their cars for 10 years or longer; once their vehicle is paid off, the longer they can go without having another car note, the more money they'll put away. And since a car note is usually the biggest expense after mortgage or rent, the ability to skip it is tremendous in freeing up money for you to sock away.

Constantly buying new cars is expensive

Jeremy Vohwinkle says that constantly trading in and buying a new vehicle every three to five years can drain a lot of money from your account. Doing that with miniscule down payments also increases the chance that you'll end up "upside down" in your car loan. Like being "underwater" on your house, this is when you owe more on the loan than the car is worth. This can happen easily with a new car and a small down payment, because cars depreciate so quickly after you drive them off the lot. Vohwinkle says people who constantly upgrade their vehicles can find themselves in a "neverending cycle" of upside-down loans, leaving you lacking in funds for your other expenses. "All of that extra money you're saving by not having a car note could go to your retirement accounts or to pay off debt. You really should only think about a new car when reliability becomes an issue," he says.

No car note=money in the bank every month

Look at it this way: No longer making a $250 car note payment every month means saving $3,000 per year. And if you pay yourself with that $250 every month and earn 4 percent on it, you'll have $17,000 at the end of five years. If you can manage to hang onto that car for ten years and bank that $250 you're saving and earn 4 percent on it, you'll have more than $37,000 put away. Even if you have to sink $3,000 in repairs and maintenance on that vehicle during those ten years, you'll still end up with $34,000.

Then, from all those savings, you can take $25,000 buy a new vehicle and still have $9,000 left over in the bank. It sounds simple, but so many of us are just so tempted by new vehicles with state-of-the-art amenities that we drive down to the car lot to trade in our perfectly-working vehicle with 65,000 miles on it. We may trade up to the newest big hit, but we take a huge hit as well—in our long-term wallets.

At least 100,000 miles

Aim to drive your vehicle to at least 100,000 miles, if not more. Most modern vehicles made today are made to run longer than that (an article at About.com estimates most can make it to 150,000). As cars get older, they do require maintenance and repairs, so be realistic. Help keep your car on the road as long as possible by: following the maintenance schedule, keeping a repair fund, fixing things as soon as they break, shopping around for a good mechanic, and using quality replacement parts.

Can you hang onto a car too long? Of course. If the car becomes unreliable or your repairs cost more than it's worth, by all means visit the car lot. And while we advocate driving your vehicle as long as you can, there's no need to deprive yourself of a decent set of wheels. If you truly have your financial house in order, no debt, substantial retirement savings, an emergency fund and a decent down payment, then buy a new car in a few years if that's what you want. Just understand that you're making sacrifices in other areas of your financial life.

For some, 200,000 miles is the new 100,000 miles

With advances in engineering and proper maintenance, many of today's vehicles can be driven more than 200,000 miles. The U.S. Department of Transportation says the average life of a vehicle is 12 years or 128,500 miles. And, Consumer Reports says many vehicles can go even further until they need engine rebuilding.

Keep a clean driving record

It pays to keep a clean driving record. According to an article in Bankrate.com, a traffic violation can cost you not just the fine but up to $700 more in insurance premiums over the next three years. That's because after one violation, most insurance companies will raise your premiums by an average of 20 percent. So that $200 speeding ticket you got may ultimately drain up to $900 out of your pocket. (And God forbid you get another ticket.)

Fight it or try a no contest plea

A history of driving infractions could mean tens of thousands of dollars over the course of a decade in fines and higher insurance premium. If you do get a ticket for any reason, be sure to fight it— or at least try. According to the National Motorists Association, an advocacy group for drivers, fewer than 5 percent of offenders fight their traffic tickets. But in actuality there are number of tactics you can use to try to minimize the damage, or at least prevent it from going on your record where your insurer will discover it. For example, most jurisdictions expect drivers to quickly pay traffic fines and move on. But according to some experts, by merely showing up in court and taking a few steps, you stand a good chance of reducing the fine—and perhaps getting out of the ticket altogether. Also, many jurisdictions have special "no contest" pleas for first-time offenders. This often will keep the ticket off your driving record and may pave the way for a reduced fine. Call the court and ask.

Traffic court is a game, so learn how to play it

Traffic courts are designed on the basis that the overwhelming majority of offenders simply will pay their tickets and move on. With hundreds of cases moving through a traffic court every day, there simply aren't enough funding, staffing and time to prosecute cases and take them to trial. So merely showing up to court can make a big difference. "By simply showing up, a lot of things can happen in your favor. You give yourself a lot of leverage by contesting [a traffic violation]," says Gary Biller, executive director of the National Motorists Association.

Alex Carroll, author of "Beat the Cops," says that in busy traffic courts, prosecutors often will meet in hallways to strike plea deals to cut down on the number of cases. These offers could include a big discount on your traffic fine or a promise that this ticket won't appear on your driving record, Carroll says. If this doesn't happen, try to reschedule the trial, increasing the likelihood that the police officer who caught you won't show up in court. If the cop is a no-show, that may result in dismissal of your case, since you have the legal right to question your accuser.

Carroll also recommends filing a "discovery of motion" to request everything about your case, from the officer's notes to calibration certificates for the radar gun that clocked you doing 50 m.p.h. in a 35 m.p.h. zone. Then, be sure to document the alleged infraction yourself. Take photos of the traffic scene and collect any other evidence that supports your stance. Another option is to fight the ticket by mail—a "trial by declaration." Carroll says a "reasonable, coherent argument" often can end up in a dismissal, as police officers are unlikely to submit written rebuttal.

Whatever you do, don't just bow down to a ticket. It can have surprising long-lasting impacts that can hurt you financially. It's worth putting up a fight, even if you were in the wrong. And although this goes without saying for reasons that go beyond financial, don't drink and drive—the impacts of a DWI can add up to a whopping $20,000 when it's all over.

CHAPTER 8

CONSPICUOUS CONSUMPTION: HE WHO APPEARS TO HAVE THE MOST OFTEN HAS THE LEAST

"My favorite things in life don't cost any money. It's really clear that the most precious resource we all have is time."

—*Steve Jobs*

If there's one thing we Americans do well with money, it's that we spend it.

It's one thing when celebrities and rich people do these kinds of things but it's another when middle class people start spending outside of their income limits.

We can try all we want but we're never going to live that life. We're never going to be like Paris Hilton, we're never going to live like Jay Z and despite what we may see on our favorite sitcoms, we can't go out every night of the week, work as a plumber and live in a nice big house. Hollywood has overbuilt our expectations of what life should be.

Face it, you're a regular Joe or a Regular Jane. You make $41,300 per year, you drive a Toyota Corolla, you shop at Wal-mart, you use coupons to buy Dominoes Pizza and there are times when you can't go out on the weekend because you don't have any money. You have a degree in General Studies, $5,000 in the bank and you mow you own lawn or you do your own nails. You're never going to drive a Ferrari, you're never going to vacation in the Hamptons and you're never going to be a rock star and you're never going to walk down a red carpet.

That's okay. We don't have to have or do these things to live a fulfilling life. The problem is that people with overblown desires to live the life they *wish* they could have is going to degrade the good things about their life that they *certainly* could have. Many people who would otherwise have a solid foot in the middle class spend themselves right out of the picture. According to the Census Bureau, we spend $1.33 for every dollar we earn. Spending money we don't have to try to live a life we'll never live is like hanging onto the edge of a cliff and reaching for an imaginary pile of money. It's all a mirage, and at some point we're going to lose our grip and fall. Our willingness to accept the confines of your middle class lifestyle is one of the most important parts of financial security.

Sure, it's nice to have a bunch of luxuries. But unless we have an unlimited about of money in the bank, buying these things when we don't have the money only digs our hole deeper. We're ultimately making ourselves poorer and actually moving ourselves further from the lifestyle we want.

"You might have a lot of stuff now and a great life today, but if you're doing it all by borrowing and building up debt, the bill is going to come due someday," says Adam Koos, financial advisor and president of Libertas Wealth Management. "When it does, life can get pretty miserable and depressing."

As millions of Americans find out every year, it might be better to have not known luxury than to go from living in luxury to living in poverty. If you live beyond your means and support that lifestyle with credit cards and debt, it will always come back to get you. It may not be this year, next year or even five years from now, but if you're making $40,000 per year and you're spending $45,000 per year, at some point you will pay that difference.

And you will pay it back tenfold—because you're more than likely making up that difference with 20 percent interest. At that point, you're lifestyle is going to be *worse* than had you just learned to live on the income you already had.

The best thing to do is not even start down that path in the first place. Danny Kofke, the schoolteacher who documented supporting his family of four on only $40,000 per year, says that unless you've got a big income, making sacrifices and learning to do without some luxuries is one of the only ways to build financial security.

"We didn't buy into the hype of spending our entire paycheck. I think more people are starting to realize those material things don't always buy you happiness," says Kofke. "Your neighbors across the street may have all of these nice things, but you don't know if they're up all night wondering if they can keep up with the bills."

A major part of gaining financial stability is mastering your purchasing. And a major part of that is having a strong understanding of *needs* versus *wants,* then learning how to balance and manage your purchases between the two. A person may want a BMW, a jet ski, $200 concert tickets and a trip to Vegas. But do they *need* them? No. They'll get by just fine with a Toyota, a bike from Wal-Mart and perhaps a cheap kayak from the sporting goods store. It may seem like you're depriving yourself of things, but you're really just substituting overpriced luxuries that you can't afford with reasonable and rational options that you can afford. And you're also allowing yourself to put a little more money away in the process.

We're not saying you have to completely sell yourself short and can't enjoy any luxuries in life. The trick is to learn where to splurge and how much to splurge relative to your income. If you're 35 years old, bringing home $150,000 per year, have a modest $2,000 mortgage payment, $72,000 set aside for retirement, no credit card debt and no kids, then yes, you can likely swing that $700 monthly note on a new BMW. But if you're earning $60,000 a year, have two kids, no emergency fund, no retirement savings and only $5,000 in liquid assets to your name, plus a few thousand in credit card debt, then you had better opt for a used Toyota.

Don't think of what you're giving up; think of what you're getting—financial security. That means going to bed every night knowing that you're prepared for any unforeseen troubles down the road. It won't be the end of the world if you lose your job, the stock market crashes or your car gets stolen. Sure, those things suck, but you'll have money in the bank to help get you through it.

Kimberly Foss, founder of Empyrion Wealth Management, says frivolous spending and consumption is usually rooted in instant gratification. The biggest problem is that most people who over-spend usually use debt to finance their purchases because they don't have the cash to support the purchase in the first place. The fancy car, the brand-name clothes and the endless splurges are paid for with debt.

"That immediate gratification lasts 15 seconds, and the debt can last a lifetime. People have to control the urge to buy those im-pulse items because once they get into that lifestyle the debt just accumulates," she says.

Sonya Britt, President of the Financial Therapy Association, says people often buy things they can't afford because they feel they are missing out. Whether it's an iPad for $600, the newest Play-station for $300 or $2,000 for the latest and greatest in televisions, there is a desire to keep up with the crowd. And it's not just teen-agers and twentysomethings that do it. Gen Xers and Baby Boomers fund purchases beyond their means with credit cards and home equity loans.

"It's ultimately about peer pressure. [Some] people feel like they need to stay with the herd. Others adapt new technologies as soon as they can regardless of the price because they feel they have to be an innovator and stay out in front," says Britt.

The question is, how much are you willing to give up and sacrifice later down the line to have some of these luxuries now? Are you willing to work until you're 75? Are you willing to downsize to a smaller home in retirement? Are you willing to tell your children you can't take them to Disney World because you had to have leather seats and a sunroof in your car? Not considering how these things could impact life later on makes for a dim future. Paying a $650 monthly car note and socking away only $75 per month in your child's education fund may not be the best use of money.

"You need to have some sort of visualization of what your life will look like in the future. You can have the BMW now, but you're not going to be able to send your kids to college and you're going to have to retire a lot later," says Britt.

Much of our conspicuous consumption is driven by the media. And it's not just hip-hop stars and athletes who have kids spending $6,000 on rims for their vehicles. It's sitcoms, movies, and regular mainstream entertainment that constantly embeds things in your mind about what middle-class life is supposed to be like. "You turn on the television for a 30-minute show, and you have 15 minutes of advertisements telling you what you have to have," Britt says. "Then you're bombarded by ads on the Internet. We are constantly bombarded by the media telling us what we need to have to be happy. People measure and compare themselves by what they see on television."

The first part of throwing away less of your money is to simply educate yourself and realize the consequences of doing so. Unless you take an active approach and learn about your overspending and how it is impacting you, you're always going to buy into the temptation to buy the latest and greatest of everything. J.D. Roth says we live in a culture that makes us spend money. "We have a system in which advertising and marketing are so powerful and influential that we can not even appreciate their power and influence," he says. "People say it has no impact on them but companies are spending billions per year to figure out how to influence you on levels you can't even appreciate."

Stop spending money to impress others

When you see a person driving an impressive car, wearing nice clothes and spending money at upscale establishments, you're usually inclined to believe they're rich. It's not always the case. For many people, those signs of wealth simply mask a financial struggle that is going on behind closed doors.

William Hammer, Jr., certified financial planner and executive vice president of Vanderbilt Wealth Management, says you should focus more on invisible wealth than visible wealth. "Visible wealth" is the cars, the house, the fancy outings, the name-brand items and the spending of money that people can see. That's okay if you're truly rich and can afford these things, but Hammer says that most visible wealth is a house of cards and that most people don't have the assets or money to back it up. "We know that most people don't have money behind that. A lot of people have visible wealth and I'd say only one out of three of them actually have money," says Hammer.

The others, he says, are buried up to their eyeballs in debt or spending their money as fast as they can earn it. At some point the hen will come home to roost. And then that house of cards is going to crumble, revealing that behind those fancy cars and name-brand clothes they were broke. Hammer says it's important to learn at an early age that conspicuous consumption and material things does not always equate to wealth or financial security.

Financial security is having money in the bank to take care of emergencies and funds set aside for retirement. It is having no or little debt, being able to sleep well at night and not having to worry about how you're going to pay the bills. But real wealth like this and the financial security that comes with it is invisible. Unless you're walking around showing people your account statements, no one is going to see or know about it. For some, this is a hard concept to grasp because it runs so against the Hollywood culture.

"I think you have to start out early on thinking about your culture of money, and you need to discuss this with your family. I would rather have invisible wealth that my friends don't know about," says Hammer. "Some people spend their whole life trying to accumulate the visible wealth thinking they're doing well—and by the time they realize they have no money, it's too late."

Think about it: Spending money to impress others means you're ultimately spending that money on them, not yourself. It's also temporary because if you keep doing it, the bills are going to catch up with you at some point, your house of cards is going to fall, and everyone will discover that in all those years you were living beyond your means, and on borrowed time.

Get educated on money matters

Most conspicuous consumption is ultimately rooted in a lack of knowledge on money matters. Few people would dig their financial graves if they actually knew they were doing so. The fact that you're reading this book demonstrates that you're trying to learn more about personal finance. You don't have to become an expert to get your financial house in order, but many Americans lack the knowledge to optimize their financial situations.

The 2011 National Consumer Financial Literacy Survey polled 1,000 adults and found that only 43 percent had a budget to keep track of how much they spend on food, housing and entertainment. Only 68 percent said they paid their bills on time and have no debts in collection; 33 percent said they have no savings. Sixty-seven percent of people said they save less than 10 percent of their income for retirement (32 percent save nothing), and 65 percent had not ordered a copy of their credit report in the past 12 months.

But things can get worse. According to a paper by the National Bureau of Economic Research, which surveyed 1,500 Americans in the summer of 2009, less than 10 percent of respondents were able to answer correctly a list of questions about economics and finance in everyday life correctly. Half said they had trouble keeping up with bills, and only half had emergency funds set aside to cover three months' worth of living expenses. Twenty-three percent of those surveyed also said they had used some type of high-cost borrowing like payday loan stores and pawn shops.

Only 42 percent said they had tried to figure out how much to save for retirement, and only 51 percent had a retirement account through an employer. About 20 percent of respondents who had auto loans didn't know the interest rate they were paying.

How has this happened? Part of the problem starts in our schools. We teach our kids how to measure the circumference of a rectangle and make them memorize the table of elements but unless the teacher goes out of his or her way to do so, we don't teach them how to balance a checkbook or calculate an interest charge. The 2011 Teens and Money Survey released by Charles Schwab & Co., Inc., revealed that teens aren't learning much about personal finance. While they're aware of the economic problems their parents may be facing, only 35 percent know how to balance a checkbook. Only 25 percent of those surveyed understood whether a check cashing service is good to use and only 32 percent said they know how credit card interest and fees work. While 82 percent of teens said their parents have taught them the basics of money management, it doesn't rank too high on the list. Among the general topics that parents talk to their teens about a lot, the survey found that the top topics were college costs (65 percent) and cleaning their room (59 percent). Smart money management skills were further down the list, tucked between conversations about drugs and alcohol and dating/sex.

"Money management is arguably one of the most important skills people can learn growing up. In most schools you get virtually no exposure to even the most basic personal finance education," says Andrew Schrage, editor of Moneycrashers.com.

The big problem isn't that our teens don't know much about money. It's that they graduate high school and then go on to college not knowing about money. And you know what often happens in college—racking up student loans, piling on credit card debt and reckless spending. Unless they're majoring in finance and running amortization schedules, they don't learn much more about money management in college. Before you know it they're 40 years old and still never learned about the concept of compound interest or how making the minimum payment on your credit card can dramatically increase the amount of debt you'll have to pay.

"Many people might not learn these things until they're in their 30s or 40s... until they get into serious debt or [have] financial problems. And at that point it's a little too late," says Schrage.

One has to wonder if our retail-driven country and power brokers designed it this way intentionally. Imagine the pain retailers would feel if people suddenly started living within their means. Traffic at malls would go down substantially. Upscale brands would be forced to drop their prices, or maybe even go bankrupt. Pawn shops and payday loan centers would disappear. The auto accessory industry might see revenues plummet by 90 percent. Massive homes all over the country would go unsold, status-symbol cars would rust away on the dealership lots and E-Trade would see 50 million new IRA accounts opened within the course of a week. Our robust economy owes a lot of its success to financially unconscious people spending money they don't have.

So people end up in the real world without the proper personal finance education to make the right rational decisions. And the next thing you know they're in a house they can't afford with a mortgage they can't understand. They're upside down in their vehicle because they listened to the dealer who talked them into putting little money down and stretching out the loan to six years. They have no health insurance, meager savings, no retirement accounts, and a mass of credit card debt. The worst part is that they think they're doing fine because they have a nice home, a new car and everything they "want."

You don't need to take a class to learn this stuff; you can educate yourself over time. Reading this book is a great start. Then get a few more books. Subscribe to a personal finance magazine or two like *Money* or *Kiplinger's Personal Finance*. Visit web sites like Moneycrashers.com, Interest.com or Bankrate.com. Take an interest and inform yourself.

Don't go broke chasing technology

You know the routine. You buy the newest, highest-megapixel, highest-rated camera for $1,200—and six months later, it's outdated and on sale for $800. Technology changes so much that if you try to keep up with it, you'll be upgrading your televisions, cameras and computers more than you change underwear.

Millions of people do this every year and drive themselves straight into financial ruin. When we keep upgrading your tech toys, we're not only spending money on things we don't need, we're buying rapidly-depreciating items that will be barely worth half their cost in less than a year. And even when we buy the latest, coolest device, doesn't it always seem like the upgrade comes out a month later for $10 more?

New technologies are always around the corner. When you upgrade, you're throwing away money that you could have kept had you just hung on to what you had. The only ones who are winning are the tech companies. Of course, we're not suggesting hanging on to your cassette players and shoe-sized phones. We're just saying that you should think hard about why and when you upgrade. In general, you should upgrade when you can afford to and when the added benefits of the technology meet your needs. If you're upgrading to an expanded phone service just because it allows you to play movies on your phone, think about whether you really need it.

You should especially consider upgrading when a device breaks. If your television crapped out then by all means, buy the biggest and best one you can for your budget, because (if you're paying any attention to what we're saying), you know you will be holding onto that television for at least ten years.

Unless you've got unlimited funds or have a work-related reason for it, don't be an "early adopter"—people who stand in lines and camp out to have the newest device when it comes out. It's a bad, bad idea that not only ensures you'll pay the highest price but also runs the risk that you'll have a device where all the kinks haven't been worked out.

When you chase technology and use gadgets as a trophy or source of pride, you will never be satisfied because there is something better every week. You're always going to be buying, not out of necessity for the gadgets themselves, but because of the necessity to keep up with the Joneses. You'll eventually end up with a closet of outdated computers, cameras, and phones alongside a mounting credit card bill or a declining bank account balance.

Avoid overspending on cell phones

We have to bring up cell phones because they're such a money drag for some people, especially the younger set. If you're making $35,000 a year and you're spending $250 a month on your cell phone bill, that's almost 10 percent of your annual income. That's how much money you should be putting away every month. Of course you need a phone, but can't you scrimp by on a $79 monthly plan?

According to a survey by JD Power & Associates, the average cell phone bill in the U.S. in 2008 was $78. That is $936 per year. Even with discounts, a family of four could spend well over $2,500 per year on cell phone services. That's not small change when you consider that half of Americans also report they would be unable to come up with $2,000 to cover an emergency if they needed to. Schwark Satyaholu of Billshrink.com says the average American consumer overspends on their cell phone expenses by $300 per year. Eight out of 10 people also do not use what they pay for. So think about what services you get and how much you spend. Do you really need to pay extra to play games, watch movies and listen to music on your phone? Can you get by on the minimum-cost data plan? If you must upgrade, at least until your contract renews; you can often get the phone for a third of what it would cost otherwise.

Take the iPhone 4s at Verizon. As of March 2012, they ran a reasonable $199 with a 2-year contract. But those who couldn't wait until their contract expired had to pay the full retail price of $649. It sounds unfathomable but many consumers do just that, because they can't wait. Learn to wait. Buy a decent phone at the discount rate, get insurance on it and learn to live with it for the next two years. You'll save yourself a lot of money. One other option can be to try calling your cell phone company when you're within three months of your renewal date. If you call and threaten to move to another carrier, they will often waive the remaining time on your contract and let you renew now. That will get you the phone at the contract price. It doesn't always work, but it's worth a try.

Know the traditional personal finance rules of thumb

Following some of the traditional personal finance rules of thumb will help you make better money decisions in your everyday life. It may also help you avoid spending so much on things you don't really need.

You'll find most of the traditional rules laid out throughout this book, but we'll give them here to you in one list. Like anything, they're flexible, but they give you a general ballpark of where you should be when you are considering a financial decision:

- You should spend no more than three times your household salary on a house. So, if you're making $60,000 per year, you shouldn't spend more than $180,000 on a house. (Unfortunately it may not even be possible to live by this rule in some high-priced housing markets nowadays.)

- Your mortgage should be no more than two times your household income. So, if you're making $60,000 per year, you should not carry more than $120,000 in mortgage debt.

- Your maximum mortgage payments, including taxes and insurance, should be no more than 28 percent of your gross monthly salary.

- Your maximum for all debt payments, including your mortgage, car note, home equity line of credit cards and student loans, should be no more than 36 percent of your gross monthly salary.

- You should save 10 percent of your take-home pay, in addition to your retirement plans, for other savings and financial goals. MSN Money writer Liz Weston says if you're young that 10 percent will only cover the basics. You should save "15 percent for comfort, 20 percent to escape."

- You should have a life insurance policy that covers between six and 10 times your family income. So, if you have a household income of $80,000, you should carry between $480,000 and $800,000 in life insurance.

- To find out how much of your retirement portfolio should be invested in stocks, subtract your age from 120. So, if you're 35 years old, you should have 85 percent of your retirement funds in stocks.

- You should drive your vehicle for at least ten years, or until it becomes unreliable. Or you start spending more than 20 percent of its value per year on maintenance and repairs.

- When buying a vehicle, the 20/4/10 rule of thumb says you should put at least 20 percent down, finance for no more than four years and the monthly payment should be less than 10 percent of your income.

- To determine the five-year true cost to own a new vehicle in monthly terms (including depreciation, interest, fuel costs, taxes, insurance, maintenance and repairs), take the vehicle's price tag, double it and divide by 60. So, for a $25,000 vehicle, the true monthly cost to own is $833.

- You should aim to have 20 times your gross annual income to retire comfortable. Remember, this is your average gross income. You may start your career making $30,000 per year but may well be making $100,000 by the time you retire. So, split it down the middle and say $65,000 per year. That means you should aim to retire with $1.3 million to maintain your lifestyle.

- To withdraw from your portfolio for up to 40 years, you can usually safely withdraw up to 4 percent of its value every year.

- When you have to repair an appliance, you should generally buy a new one if it is more than 8 years old, according to Consumer Reports.

- When you get a financial windfall, use 1-2 percent to treat yourself. Depending on your financial situation, this could be a little low. If you're 30 years old with no credit card debt, a decent amount of savings and are living well within your means, you shouldn't feel bad about spending up to 10 percent of a windfall on something fun for yourself.

- According to the book *The Millionaire Next Door*, your net worth should be equal to your age times your pretax income divided by 10. So, if you're 35 years old making $40,000 per year, your net worth should be about $140,000. This includes all of your assets (including home) minus your liabilities and debts. (Although in today's real estate market with depressed housing values, many people don't match up to this formula.)

- You should not borrow more in student loans to go to college than you expect to make your first year out of school. So, if you're expecting to make $35,000 per year when you first graduate, don't let your student loans top that amount.

- The most you should pay for a car is typically one-half your gross annual income. So, if you make $40,000 per year, you should not be spending more than $20,000 on a vehicle.

- Inflation typically runs 3.43 percent per year. That means that prices typically double every 20 years in terms of real money. This should stress the importance of saving and earning a return on your money. Because without any interest, the

$10,000 you have in the bank now will really only be worth $9,657 next year. And in 20 years, it will only be worth $5,000 in real dollars.

- You should invest no more than 10 percent of your total savings in your employer's stock. The reason for this is diversification. You already make your living with your employer and have a large financial stake vested there. The last thing you want is a large chunk of your portfolio there too. Should the company have some financial issues, you're risking not only your job but your investments.

- The long-term average of the stock market is about 10 percent. But many experts, including Warren Buffet, expect returns to be much lower over the next few decades. Seven percent is a more conservative bet.

- To figure out how long it will take for an investment to double, divide 72 by the annual return. So, if you're earning 6 percent on your money, you'll typically double your money every 12 years.

Save money on everyday purchases and bank the difference

Since one of the only ways to build wealth and improve your financial situation is to spend less, learning to live frugally can be pretty important. That's because if you save the difference, it can help build up your funds over time. Leah Ingram, author of *Suddenly Frugal: How to Live Happier and Healthier for Less*, says you really can't start to save real money until you can first identify where you are spending it.

Ingram recommends you first look at your credit and debit card statements and knock out any automatic deductions for subscriptions or services you may not be using anymore. Then, make sure you're not paying any late fees and extra charges due to "financial sloppiness" and not paying your bills on time.

"Most people can easily locate and find $100 a month or more in waste. It starts to give you a sense of how all these things can add up," she says.

When you start going over your bills and see where the money is going out, you can then start to identify where you might be spending too much money. Being frugal is not about being cheap or a tightwad. It's simply about getting more out of your money. Why would you pay $38 for your groceries when you could get them for $32? Why would you pay $52 for a pair of pants when you could get them for $40? Looking for sales, discounts and other ways to save is simply about getting the most bang for your buck and the most value for your dollar.

The key is that when you save money you use those savings not to buy more stuff but to save and invest the difference. If you manage to trim some fat out of your budget or use a variety of frugal living tactics to save $150 per month, that's $1,800 per year you're saving. If you actually put those funds away every month, you'd have $9,000 in five years. And if you were able to earn a 5 percent return on those funds, you'd have $10,300 in five years. Keep that up for ten years and you'd have almost $24,000, and in 20 years you'd have more than $62,000. Saving a few bucks here and there and banking the difference can add up big over time.

Ingram says there is some truth to the idea that the rich are rich "because they pinch pennies. Some people might live frugally because they have to do it to make ends meet, but many people just want to live better on less money," she says. Some of the easiest ways to start saving, she adds, is to cut back on coffee shop trips and to start brown-bagging your lunch. Grabbing a $2-3 cup of Joe at Starbucks every morning can add up to over $600 per year. And switching from an $8 daily lunch to bringing your own or packing leftovers from the previous night's dinner can save up to $2,000 per year. The options are limitless. (You can find more about living frugally at www.suddenlyfrugal.com.)

Learn to negotiate

Learning to negotiate on price can come in handy when you buy a car or a house, but Michael Friedman, management consultant and creator of the economics blog *The Behaviorist*, said just about anything these days is negotiable. Whether it's your cell phone company, a caterer for a wedding, a gym membership or even retail, especially in a down economy, the price isn't always set in stone. "So many things today are negotiable that you normally would not think about. That includes anything from suits to insurance policies and cell phone contracts," says Friedman.

Don't pay full price

When businesses aren't selling their products or services at full capacity, they're more likely to look at price in terms of what they *can* get, not what they want to get. So if a furniture store is asking $2,900 for a bedroom set and you tell them you can only pay $2,700, they're likely going to think hard about if they want to let that sale get away for a measly $200—because at that point, their only options are $2,700 from you or nothing at all.

And they're more inclined to come down on the price if business has been slow and that particular bedroom set hasn't been moving. They still have to make a profit on it so they're not going to sell it below cost, but even if your negotiations only knock off $100, that's better than nothing. It's $100 you didn't have to work for. And if you get shot down then, what have you really lost?

You're more likely to make negotiations work at smaller stores. It's highly unlikely you could walk into Walmart or Best Buy and convince the manager to knock $100 off that $900 television. You can't get Domino's to knock another $5 off your pizza and you can't expect Starbucks to give you a latte for half price. Their sales volume is so high they don't have to negotiate, and for big retailers their price cuts usually come in the form of weekly sales anyway. But if you went down to the independent audio/video retailer, furniture store, flooring company or appliance store, they may very well match the price of the big-box retailer and throw in a few extras.

Cell phones and credit cards

A big spot where you should learn to negotiate is with cell phone companies. If you're a customer of Verizon, Sprint, AT&T or another major carrier, call their national customer service number and see what they can do for you. Want to upgrade but still have a year left on your contract? See a better deal and are thinking about moving to another carrier? Just call and tell them. Tell them what you want and why you are thinking about taking your business elsewhere. More often than not they will come back with some kind of offer that will at least save you a few bucks. I know it works because I've done it a number of times.

Credit card debt and interest rates are also highly negotiable. If you're paying 20 percent on a balance, have been a long-time customer and always pay your bills on time, call them and ask for a better deal. Tell them one of your other credit card companies is offering a balance transfer deal at 5 percent. Tell them you want to stick with them but you have to do what is in your own best interest. Tell them you just can't pay that 20 percent rate anymore.

It's almost a given that the person on the other end of the line will reply, "Well, let's see what we can do for you." They'll poke around their computer, put you on hold a few times and eventually come back with an offer. And it could be 12 percent. That means you're now saving a whopping 8 percent on the rate you were paying earlier. You'll be able to pay off your balance sooner and can save a bundle in interest.

You usually have to have a decent credit score to do this, but it works. And yes, it's really that simple; all you have to do is call. Friedman says many people shy away from trying to negotiate because they feel it will turn into an uncomfortable experience or that they are scared they'll be rejected. That's just not the case—there are many companies that expect and deal with this every day.

Medical bills

You may not realize that you can also negotiate medical bills. Few patients ever do it but the amount you are billed for is not always the amount you have to pay. Jeremy Vowhikle says you should be proactive and figure out the fair-market price of the procedures you received, and then talk to someone in the billing department. Hospitals are used to being stiffed on their bills and are used to billing for as much as they can, so there's likely a lot of wiggle room in those numbers. And from their point of view, they may very well take $4,200 for a $5,000 bill if they can get the money right then and there. Their only other options may be accepting payment months late, moving you to an extended payment plan or you walking away altogether. "The idea of having to be shrewd and aggressive makes some people feel uncomfortable," Vowhikle says. "Sometimes negotiations can be graceful, but there can be a lot of haggling going on back and forth."

There are plenty of books available on negotiation, so even if you think you can't negotiate, you can teach yourself. Some of the basics include getting over your fear of negotiating, making an aggressive first offer, always making a counter offer and never taking it personally.

CHAPTER 9

SOME OTHER STUFF ABOUT MONEY

Do the math when making financial decisions

So many people throw math and logic out of the window when it comes to personal finance. It's funny how little important applicable personal finance math skills they teach in high school and college. You'll have to learn equations for calculating square roots, the circumference of a rectangle, the diameter of a circle and the rate of speed of a tricycle. But few math classes teach students about interest rates, amortization schedules, minimum payments, retroactive interest rate applications and how compounding works.

Laura Laing, author of *Math for Grownups* says that a basic mastery of math is critical in evaluating decisions that can affect your finances. Whether you're talking numbers at the car dealership, thinking about buying a home, determining how long it will take you to pay off your credit card or simply trying to find the best return on your money, you should understand basics.

"We need to be able to look at the numbers and see if it makes sense. It's not always in our best interest to trust the experts that are telling us what to do. We need to have a critical eye on these decisions," says Laing.

There's no reason to fret. Gone are the days when you had to sit down with a pen and paper, sketch out some complicated formula, carry the 1 and move the decimal two places. Today you don't even need to know the formulas but you do need to know what the formulas calculate and how to apply them. You can use a variety of online calculators or apps where you simply plug in the numbers.

When dealing with money, some of the basics you should know how to calculate include:

- Simple interest to determine how much you'll pay on a loan to borrow that money.

- Minimum payments on credit cards and the impact it has on your balance and the interest you'll pay over time.

- How long it will take you to pay off your credit card if you increase your monthly payments.

- How much you can afford to borrow and how much home you can afford.

- How much your monthly payment is going to be on an auto loan.

- How much interest you'll pay on a home over the life of the mortgage and how to generate a loan amortization schedule.

- Whether debt consolidation is right for you.

- How much you'll need to save for retirement.

- Whether or not you should refinance your mortgage and how much money you will save by doing so.

You can find calculators for all of these things at Interest.com.

You can use math and these formulas to make the optimal financial decisions and pick the best of the options you have. Laing says that before you jump into using formulas and running calculations, you should make sure that you're plugging in the right numbers.

"You may not need to know the formula but you need to know what the variables are. You need to pay close attention to what the calculator is asking you to input," says Laing.

Finally, don't just think of things in terms of a "penny saved is a penny earned." Go a step further and think that a penny you give up is a penny that could be earning interest for you. You're not just saving $100. Think that if you saved that $100 and left it parked in an account or investment that was bringing in 5 percent per year, it would be $432 in 30 years. Think long-term and then ask yourself if you really need to part with that $100.

Save big by living healthy

Staying in shape isn't just about looking good. It can save you a lot of money over the course of your life in reduced insurance premiums and fewer medical bills. You already know how much smoking can cost you. Well, living an inactive life and eating cheeseburgers for dinner every night can cost you as well.

First, being fit means lower health care costs. According to the Center for Disease Control, an overweight person who loses 10 percent of his or her body weight and keeps it off can save up to $5,300 on lifetime medical costs for hypertension, diabetes, heart disease and stroke.

Next, you could be paying more in health insurance if you buy your insurance independently and are overweight. A survey by Towers Watson consulting firm found that 12 percent of employers had programs in place in 2011 to reward or penalize employees based on their health metrics. That same survey found that by the end of 2012, 38 percent of employers were expected to have those programs in place. When employers have to foot a part of the bill for your insurance premiums they have a vested interest in you being healthy because it means they'll save money. Many employers are now moving to incentive programs so you could even *earn* money or rewards simply by maintaining your health.

Then there's life insurance. According to the Insurance Information Institute, consumers who lose a significant amount of weight could save as much as 40 percent on their life insurance premiums. And smokers? They often pay *double* the premiums of non-smokers.

Finally, there are all the increased health risks associated with being overweight and unhealthy: high cholesterol, gallstones, type 2 diabetes, high blood pressure, coronary artery disease, stroke, sleep apnea and certain types of cancer. Problems with any or all of these things can cost money. Lots of it.

Of course there's nothing to say that slim people who are in shape can't develop illnesses, but you may as well try to eliminate the risks you can. It can sometimes cost a little bit more to eat healthier, but you'll constantly recoup the added expense by realizing savings in other parts of your life.

Take risks while you're young

When we talk about taking risks we don't mean driving 120 miles per hour on the freeway or base jumping off a 45-story building. We're talking about taking highly calculated risks when there is great potential for monetary return or professional growth—like acting on a long-standing business idea or your desire to make it as a musician, write a novel or open a restaurant.

No reward without risk

You can not earn any reward in life without taking on a little risk. Remember that almost everything is a risk. Going to law school is a risk. Taking a new job is a risk. Buying a house is a risk. Getting married is a risk. There is a chance that all of these things could fail and you could be hit hard in the pocket book.

There's nothing wrong with risk if it is *calculated* and you have thought long and hard about the consequences of failure, your chances of success and what you should do to make it work. If you have a great business idea backed up with a solid business plan, a highly competitive advantage, years of research and planning and a little capital, you probably have better odds of success than if you came up with a restaurant concept in a bar one night and took out a $50,000 loan the next week, moving forward with no planning.

You can recover from mistakes and failures when you're young

The important thing is that if you are a person to take big risks, you should do this earlier in your life. It's easier to take some of these risks when you're in your late 20s and early 30s or before you have a family to support. You can afford to take a hit or two when you're young and still have time to make it up.

Robert Henderson says he comes across clients on occasion who are in their 60s, have amassed a large amount of wealth, then decided to risk it on a business idea they've been dreaming about since they were 20. In most cases at that point, it's just too late.

"When you've come that far—you make a mistake, open a business that doesn't work and lose it all—you just don't have any choices left. If you're 30 years old, have accumulated $50,000 and want to open a business and it tanks, you still have time to make it up," he says.

A single 30-year-old can take on far more risk than a 45-year-old with three kids. So take advantage of your situation. David Weliver, publisher of MoneyUnder30.com, says you can take more risks when you are younger because you don't have as much to lose and, in most cases, you don't have as many expenses. It's easier to take professional and career risks when you don't have a mortgage to pay and a family to support.

"If you fail when you are single, you can pretty much pick yourself up, dust yourself off and get going again. When you have a family and other financial obligations, there's a lot more collateral damage if you fail," says Weliver.

Take on healthy risk in your investments

You should also keep this in mind when investing or saving. It has been a rough decade for stocks but if you're 30 years old sitting out of the market and putting your money in CDs earning 2 percent because you think it's safe, you're making a big mistake. First of all, you're not even keeping up with inflation. But the biggest problem is that you're not taking a little risk at a time when you should be. At this point in your life, you should have at least 70-80 percent of your portfolio invested in stocks because you have time on your side to weather the risks. You might be taking on more risk but you've got a lot more time to play catch-up in your portfolio if it tanks.

"You just have a lot more time to recover. Not that you want to [fail], but you can better afford to fail once or twice when you're young than when you're further down the line," says Weliver.

Build a nest egg simply by quitting smoking

It doesn't matter when you started, how much you smoke, what it smells like or where you smoke. From a financial point of view, smoking drains enormous amount of money from your bank account due to the cost of cigarettes and health issues.

It's expensive and adds up to tens of thousands over time

At an average cost of $4 per pack, and double that in some cities, if you smoke a pack per day, you are spending $1,460 per year on cigarettes alone. Smokers typically pay 20 percent more for health insurance, too, and up to 100 percent more for life insurance. Whereas a non-smoker of the same age and health might pay $250 per year for a $250,000, 20-year policy, a smoker is likely to pay $500…or more! According to the American Cancer Society, average additional health care costs for smokers run $500 per year.

Excluding the increased costs for health insurance, that comes up to $2,210 per year to keep the habit. Over 10 years that's $22,100; over 20 years, it's $44,200. If you diverted those funds to an investment and made a conservative 4 percent on it, that's over $73,000 in 20 years. And that doesn't even include the threat that you'll develop a serious cancer someday that could cost tens of thousands of dollars. Or the other costs such as loss of productivity.

Is it really worth it?

The thing about cigarettes is this. You don't *need* them. You need to eat, you need a place to live, you need electricity, you need a phone. But you don't need to smoke. You can look for all kinds of ways to make cutbacks and save money but few things will produce instant results like quitting smoking.

Expect life to get harder

When thousands of protesters started taking to the streets of American cities in September 2011 for the Occupy Wall Street protest, it brought to light the things that many Americans have known for years—the rich are getting richer, the poor are getting poorer and the middle class is rapidly shrinking.

Middle class is shrinking

The Census Bureau also reported in September 2011 that 46.2 million Americans are now living below the poverty line. That was the highest number in the 52 years since the bureau has been publishing figures on it. It was also the first time since the Great Depression that median household income, adjusted for inflation, had not risen over such a long period. It meant that the median family is in worse shape that it was in the late 1990s. Some economists call it the "lost decade."

Even if you don't fall below the poverty line, that doesn't mean that everything's okay. The middle class is shrinking. Top earners have all the money they need to be self-sufficient and bottom earners can look to the government for assistance in the form of welfare, public housing, food stamps and grants. But for you, the regular Joe or Jane making $40,000 per year, there is nothing to help you cope with the rising costs of real estate, insurance, food and gas. Maybe you don't make enough to keep up with the costs, but you're not poor enough to help from the government. It's often called the *middle class squeeze*.

According to the Bureau of Labor Statistics, while Wall Street profits from 2007 to 2009 were up 720 percent, the unemployment rate was up 102 percent. During that time, Americans' home equity was also down 35 percent.

Be prepared

We point this out not so that you'll be cynical about your future but so that you can be realistic about it. You can only prepare for the coming hard times if you're willing to accept that they may be just around the corner. We have to face facts: we'll never be in that 1 percent. Numerically, we'll likely end up in that 99 percent of "have-nots" that we hear about.

But within that so-called "99 percent," many people get by just fine. It's better to be in the top 50 percent of the have-nots than the bottom 50 percent of the have-nots. While you still might struggle in retirement for some of the finer things you'd like, life might not be that bad. But you do have to make a conscious decision to accept that as a possibility in your future and that you—and only you—can improve your situation.

"I do believe that we're becoming more a world of haves and have-nots. The middle class is shrinking and you can not depend on the government. You need to be accountable for yourself," says Kimberly Foss.

Don't count on government to help you

You may want to tell yourself that Social Security might not be there for you. That the value of your home is going to decline in the coming years. That your insurance premiums are going to go up even more. That you're going to earn less on your portfolio. That the price of gas may rise even further. That tax rates may even increase. Tell yourself these things because it will motivate your future financial decisions to put yourself in a better position to weather the storm. After all, you can't prepare for a storm if you refuse to acknowledge that it's coming. And if you don't think these things will happen, then what have you lost? Nothing. You've only gained money because you'll now get your Social Security check *in addition* to all the money you've saved.

Despite what the Occupy Wall Street protesters may have you thinking, no one can or will help you in your economic woes except for yourself. Fortune 500 corporations aren't going to apologize for their greed and send you a compensatory reparation check for $10,000 tomorrow. The government isn't going to save you or protect you. You are on your own.

The American dream is still there, but it's a scaled-down version of what it used to be, and you're going to have to work harder for it. The American dream is now a smaller home, a more realistic vehicle, more savings, less spending, fewer toys and more awareness about why we need to avoid debt and save more. David Weliver, publisher of MoneyUnder30.com, believes the past decade will leave a lasting impression on many Gen Xers and Gen Yers.

"I think people will realize that they will have to deal with their money better, and you're not going to see as much of the rampant consumerism that we saw during the height of the housing bubble," says Weliver.

The bottom line is that shit may get harder in the future, so you have to be prepared to deal with it. And the only way you can do that is by better learning to manage your money, spend less and save more.

Marry the right person

This is easier said than done. Ideally you want to stay with the person you marry forever, but that doesn't always happen. You can do everything right, marry the person you love and in 23 years you may find out that you want to part amicably, divorce and head your separate ways.

Well, that's the best-case scenario. On the other end of the spectrum, you could get married, find out it was a total mistake, withstand nasty divorce a few years later and end up owing alimony or having to part with some of your assets. Aside from the emotional damage, divorce is a huge drain on your financial well being.

According to Maritalstatus.com, a web site that covers divorce and remarriage, the average cost of a litigated divorce in the United States is about $20,000. Cheap, do-it-yourself divorces can still cost $1,500.

The point of it all is that you should think hard not just about love but your financial future before tying the knot. You should also get to know and understand your partner's financial habits and history. When you marry a person with a mountain of debt, you too are essentially assuming that debt. And when they default on that debt or don't pay their bills, it's your problem as well as theirs.

Noah Rosenfarb, a Certified Divorce Financial Advisor with Freedom Divorce Advisors, says that biggest financial issue with divorce and separation is the transition from one household to two. A $1,200 mortgage now becomes a $1,200 mortgage and a $900 rent payment for the person who moves out. Grocery bills, insurance and all kinds of day-to-day living expenses can now double. Then it gets really tricky with savings and retirement funds.

"You're going to essentially divide everything in half. A couple may have saved $250,000 over the past 15 years, and now they've got $125,000 apiece. You essentially have to start again, and it's a lot harder to save when you're now paying a new mortgage," says Rosenfarb.

This is especially troublesome when a breadwinner may have contributed a disproportionably larger share to the community assets. Someone who might have contributed 70 percent to the savings and retirement accounts now walks away with only half. That loss can be devastating for some and can take years to recover. Rosenfarb doesn't recommend people make marriage decisions based on money, but they should at least take it into consideration.

"You need to know that going in. In most parts of the country you're going to have to split it 50/50 when you break up," he says.

Rosenfarb recommends that couples discuss these things before they get married. Some couples prefer to pool all of their assets, some like to keep their own money in their own accounts and others do a combination of the two. He also says couples should consider prenuptial agreements if they think it is necessary (although the mere discussion of one can sometimes lead to an argument). Another alternative to a prenup is to document what assets each party owned before the marriage—in most states, the division of assets or money only applies to what was acquired during the marriage.

Understand and watch your credit score

FICO scores are calculated from many things in your credit report and are derived from five main factors including: payment history (35 percent), amounts owed (30 percent), length of credit history (15 percent), new credit (10 percent) and types of credit used (10 percent). Your record of paying your bills on time and not owing too much constitutes more than half of your entire score.

Having a good credit score demonstrates that you not only have credit but you know how to use it wisely. So, if you have $20,000 in available credit on your three credit cards and you have $8,000 in balances, you're using 40 percent of your available credit. If you have $12,000 in available credit on your three credit cards and you have $8,000 in balances, you're using 67 percent of your available credit. You would have a higher score in the first example because you're utilizing less of your available credit.

Be aware that your score is not affected by your income or bank accounts. You could make $100,000 per year with $2 million in the bank, but that wouldn't count for anything if you've got 3 late payments on your report. It also doesn't matter if you pay all your bills on time if you are utilizing too much of your available credit.

"A lot of people think if they just pay their bills on time, everything with their credit score will be fine and dandy. That's just not true because credit utilization is worth 30 percent," says Jeremy Maher of MyCreditRepairTips.com.

To put it as simply as possible, the best way to earn a good FICO score is to build a long credit history of paying your bills on time and utilizing as little as possible of your available credit.

Unfortunately you also need credit to build credit. While it's admirable that you don't have credit card debt and avoid debt at all costs, if you don't have a credit card or have never taken out a loan, you're going to find it hard to build your score. That's why you need to have credit in the first place. Get a couple of credit cards, use them once a year, then lock them up in your dresser. It's a start that will at least start building your report.

Maher says your credit score can affect just about everything in your life—from your employment and how much you pay for your insurance to whether or not you have to put down deposits for certain services. Like it or not, employers, insurance companies, utility companies and cell phone companies are increasingly using FICO scores to judge you. Companies use it to judge you for your ability to pay, and insurers and employers use it because in their eyes, credit scores also score your character, integrity, reliability and safety. If you have a FICO score of 550, it tells insurers that you're more likely to get in an accident and file a claim. And it tells employers that you're likely to have financial problems and perhaps are too big of a risk. It may not be fair, but it's the reality.

"It affects people in a lot of different ways, and now with this economy, employers are so particular with whom they are hiring, they are more relying on credit scores," says Maher.

On a scale of 300 to 850, the median FICO score is 723. Stats from FICO, Inc. show that 25.5 percent of the 170 million Americans with active credit accounts have scores of 599 or below. A moderate credit score is considered to be between 650 and 699, and Maher says only 25 percent of people in the United States have a credit score of over 740.

Even if you have well-established credit with a good score and don't anticipate needing to borrow any money in the future, you should still check in on your credit once a year. You can request a free credit file disclosure or report once every 12 months from each of the nationwide consumer credit reporting agencies at Annualcreditreport.com.

To get your FICO score, you're going to have to pay. It's not much, usually about $10 or so. While you're bound to have a different FICO score from each one of the reporting agencies (Equifax, Experian and TransUnion) they usually aren't too far apart. Lenders will usually pull all three scores, then take the average. If you're planning on making a big purchase, like buying a home or a new car, you might want to pull your FICO score with one of the agencies a month or two in advance. When you apply for a mortgage or auto loan, they'll also come back with your FICO scores so you'll get to take another peek then.

At some point in your working life you may get declined for credit. Or, you may get a higher interest rate than you thought you would. No one is perfect, and few people have perfect credit scores. But you should always be working to improve yours. Consumer-friendly regulations created by the Dodd-Frank Wall Street Reform and Consumer Protection Act now require lenders to justify their decision to turn you down for credit or refuse to give you the lowest possible rate. If this happens to you, take a careful look at the lender's reasons and work to improve your credit score. Here are five of the most common reasons consumers typically see when they are declined credit, and what you can do to improve your credit score for the next time you apply for a loan:

You're delinquent on existing loans.

Your payment history on everything from mortgages and utility bills to credit cards and student loans is the single most important factor in getting more credit.

This one factor makes up 35 percent of your FICO score—the most commonly used credit scoring system, created by Fair Isaac Corp. So, if you've been late with even one or two bills, it's going to hurt you.

Your credit report will show how often you've missed payment deadlines and how long you allowed a bill to languish before catching up. A payment that was 90 days late is going to hurt you more than a payment that was 30 days late.

To fix this problem, you'll need to catch up on any past-due bills and create a foolproof system for making all future payments on time. Do that and your credit score should start improving in about three months. The longer you keep up the good work, the more attractive you'll be to potential lenders.

Too many revolving accounts.

This means you have too many credit cards. The average American has six, so it's a problem if you have 13.

Don't immediately jump and close too many accounts. That can further diminish your FICO score, especially if you're closing older accounts that have established your credit history. Start with the newest cards, with the lowest available credit lines. Make sure the balance is paid in full, and close the account or transfer the balance to another card.

Tread carefully: As you close accounts, you'll also be diminishing your overall available credit. In turn, that could increase your debt utilization. Say you have a balance of $3,500 spread over two credit cards, but you have seven other credit card accounts open.

If the total lending capacity of all those credit cards is $20,000, your debt utilization is 17.5 percent. That's not bad. But if you close four of those cards and bring your total credit limit down to $7,500, you're now using 46.6 percent of your available credit. That doesn't look so hot to lenders.

You owe too much on your accounts

This means you've spent too much of your available revolving credit. Lenders usually start turning down applicants who have spent more half of the credit limit on their credit cards. The more you've spent, the more likely you are to be rejected.

The only way you can solve this problem is to pay down some of your debt. Since all of your credit cards are factored into one number, it really doesn't make a difference which card you choose. But for your own sake, start with the ones with the highest interest rates. Another more difficult option is to call a couple of your credit card companies and ask for an increase in your credit line.

Let's say you had $5,000 of debt on five cards with $8,000 available credit. If you were able to increase that available credit to $10,000, it would drop your debt utilization from 62 percent to 50 percent.

Your credit history is too short

The problem with credit is that you usually need a little credit to get credit. Sometimes it can be a challenge getting your feet off the ground, especially when you are young. If you only have one credit card that you opened six months ago, you don't have much of a history yet. Even if you've done everything right up until now and pay all of your bills, you might still be lagging.

The only thing that can help with this problem is time. Wait six months and apply again. The odds of being approved will increase.

Too many recent credit inquiries

If you apply for too much credit in too short of a period of time, lenders are bound to think you are in some kind of financial trouble. Every time you apply for credit, the bank or store pulls a copy of your credit history to review, and the fact that you are seeking more credit is added to your record. Credit inquiries can remain on your report for up to two years.

More Stuff About Money

For more *Stuff About Money* with weekly updates and articles, visit the web site at www.somestuffaboutmoney.com.

Email any questions or comments to craig@craigguillot.com

J

K

L

S

T

U

V

W